The Practitioners' Guide to Teaching Thinking Series

TECHNIQUES FOR TEACHING THINKING

WRITTEN BY

Arthur L. Costa & Lawrence F. Lowery

SERIES TITLES

TEACHING THINKING: ISSUES AND APPROACHES
TECHNIQUES FOR TEACHING THINKING
EVALUATING CRITICAL THINKING

SERIES EDITED BY

Robert J. Swartz & D. N. Perkins

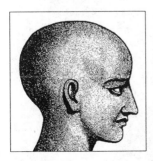

© 1989
**CRITICAL THINKING
PRESS & SOFTWARE**
(formerly Midwest Publications)
P.O. Box 448 • Pacific Grove • CA 93950-0448
Phone 800-458-4849 • FAX 408-393-3277
ISBN 0-89455-379-8
Printed in the United States of America

Chapter 4 is reprinted, with changes, from Arthur L. Costa and Robert Marzano, The language of cognition, in *Educational Leadership*, October, 1987.

Chapter 5 is reprinted from Arthur L. Costa, Mediating the metacognitive, in *Educational Leadership*, November, 1984.

Chapter 7 is reprinted, with changes, from A. Costa (Ed.), *Developing Minds: A Resource Book for Teaching Thinking*, 1985.

Permission for reprinting the three articles is granted by the publisher, the Association for Supervision and Curriculum Development., Alexandria, VA.

PURPOSE

The purpose of this book is to provide information and ideas for:

STAFF DEVELOPERS and TEACHER EDUCATORS, as they consider program content to prepare teachers to teach thinking skills.

TEACHERS, as they assess their own abilities to create classroom conditions for thinking and their readiness to implement a curriculum for developing thinking skills.

CURRICULUM DEVELOPERS, as they decide how the curriculum should be organized and sequenced according to children's developmental levels.

ADMINISTRATORS, as they assess and provide leadership for improving the conditions in their schools and classooms, which allows the stimulating teaching of thinking.

This book is intended to address some of the issues in teaching thinking discussed in the first volume (Swartz and Perkins, 1989) of this series, to build upon some of the approaches outlined in that work, and to elaborate these in new ways that we feel will be of help to practitioners working at all levels of education today.

CONTENTS

           Strategy Directly   **75**

       Why Teach Thinking Directly   76

       Process as Content   78

       When to Teach a Thinking Skill Directly   78

       A Lesson-planning Strategy for Teaching
             a Thinking Skill Directly   79

       Sample Lesson for Teaching
             a Thinking Skill Directly   82

       Ways Teachers Can Add to Their Teaching
             of Thinking Skills Directly   86

       References   88

7.   How We Know Students Are
           Getting Better at Thinking   **89**

       Persistence   90

       Decreasing Impulsivity   91

       Listening to Others   91

       Flexibility in Thinking   92

       Metacognition   93

       Checking for Accuracy and Precision   93

       Questioning and Problem Posing   94

       Drawing on Past Knowledge
             and Experiences   94

       Transference Beyond the Learning Situation   95

       Precision of Language and Thought   96

       Using All the Senses   96

       A Sense of Humor   97

       Wonderment, Inquisitiveness, Curiosity,
             and the Enjoyment of Problem Solving   98

FOREWARD

Teaching for thinking has become a major agenda in schools across this country. No one, of course, doubts that in the past educators have been concerned about the quality of student thinking and have worked to improve it. Such attempts, however, have all too often fallen prey to the pressures for coverage and for learning factual information with which all teachers have to cope. Today, by contrast, teachers in many schools are learning to manage—and even modify—the demands of coverage while emphasizing the development of forms of thinking that foster learning, understanding, and critical and creative thought. This shift reaffirms the value we place on good thinking. It also underscores the need not only to continue with these attempts but to turn more of them into greater successes. It is in this spirit that we offer a series of reflective guides for educational practitioners. We believe that enough is known today about thinking and how it can be taught to put into the hands of practitioners guide books that synthesize the relevant work of leaders in this field. This series presents a systematic conception of the aims of teaching for thinking and guidelines for achieving these aims in interactions with our students.

There is a second, less upbeat reason for publishing these volumes. Like any major shift in institutional priorities, the boom in efforts to explicitly teach thinking has provoked a wide variety of disparate approaches, claims, and advocates. They all tell us what we should be aiming at in teaching thinking and how best to do it. Often, however, hidden beneath the use of more or less the same terminology are quite different goals and means. While there is a sense in which such a ferment is healthy in a young field, the danger of fadism, miscommunication, and superficiality looms large, especially when there are pressures for immediate change and publishers are eager to respond.

It is our conviction that good thinking can be taught as a normal and comfortable element of educational practice. However, this mission cannot be accomplished overnight. It requires the very same good thinking and good sense that we all espouse as goals for our students. Thus, there is a need to stand back from the details of different methodologies and develop a broader perspective in which we tolerate a multiplicity of approaches while at the same time acknowledging a common basis lodged in a clear concept of good thinking and in a set of sound principles for teaching thinking that virtually all well-founded efforts should reflect.

We have created this series as a context in which these common goals and principles can be set out in order to provide practiced guidance to the classroom teacher and school administrator. They are the ones who have to make choices about how to implement the goal of developing students' thinking. But they do not have the time to probe the research in detail or travel around the country familiarizing themselves with approaches that claim success. Where there are basic alternatives for the teacher set against this common backdrop, these are spelled out and their scope and limits clarified.

The original concept for this series developed out of the first in a succession of annual faculty seminars sponsored and supported by the Critical and Creative Thinking Program at the University of Massachusetts at Boston, held in the summer of 1985. The participants in the seminar were:

Joan Baron	Conn. State Department of Education
Rebecca van der Bogert	Groton (MA) School System
Arthur Costa	Sacramento (CA) State University
Robert Ennis	University of Illinois
Bena Kallick	Weston Woods Foundation
Arthur Millman	University of Mass. at Boston
Stephen Norris	Memorial University of Newfoundland

Richard Paul	Sonoma State (CA) University
David Perkins	Harvard University
Linda Phillips	Memorial University of Newfoundland
Stephen Schwartz	University of Mass. at Boston
Alma Swartz	Westford (MA) School System
Robert Swartz	University of Mass. at Boston
S. Lee Winocur	Costa Mesa (CA) School District
Mary Anne Wolff	North Reading (MA) School System

While the ideas developed in these books are the authors' own, their root source and the motivation for the volumes derive from this seminar. We thank all the participants for their contributions to the development of each of these volumes. We are all dedicated to making good teaching of good thinking happen in our schools and to promoting the use of the very same good thinking on the part of professional educators as they plan and carry out this teaching.

ROBERT J. SWARTZ, FOUNDER
CRITICAL AND CREATIVE THINKING PROGRAM
UNIVERSITY OF MASSACHUSETTS AT BOSTON, AND

D. N. PERKINS, CO-DIRECTOR
PROJECT ZERO
HARVARD UNIVERSITY

GENERAL EDITORS

EDITORS' PREFACE

In this volume in *The Practitioners' Guide to Teaching Thinking Series*, Professors Costa and Lowery present an in-depth analysis of successful classroom practices in teaching for thinking. Their perspective reflects a sound understanding of children and adolescents. It takes account of both the opportunities and constraints that the regular classroom teacher faces in reshaping ordinary teaching practices to make students better thinkers. Written in the spirit of this series, it is a guidebook for the educational *practitioner*.

The goals of teaching for thinking of Professors Costa and Lowery agree with those elaborated in Volume I in this series (*Teaching Thinking: Issues and Approaches*). For them, good thinking consists of a constellation of attitudes and abilities. These work together to tap the highest potentials of the human mind in its relationship to the surrounding world. It is their conviction that all classroom teachers can remake the classroom environment and their own approach to content-teaching to become proficient teachers of thinking.

This emphasis on the need for a broad—but quite manageable—transformation of teaching and of the overall classroom environment to create an atmosphere for thinking reaffirms one of the fundamental tenets of Volume I. This tenet is that teaching for thinking should not be viewed as simply adding another subject matter or set of skills that we teach in the same old way. Rather, teaching for thinking calls for a transformation of all our instruction and should be infused throughout it. It is only through well-designed classroom structures and a redefined role of the teacher in the classroom that openness to new ideas, perseverance in thinking through issues, and looking for good reasons before accepting ideas, will be promoted.

The authors similarly acknowledge another fundamental tenet of Volume I: the need for deliberately designed lessons, set in a thinking atmosphere, that are structured to teach for very specific thinking skills and abilities. This, again, is a manageable task, and Professors Costa and Lowery provide detailed guidelines and models for the classroom teacher to employ.

Before you explore the resources of this book, we would like to make a final comment about the spirit in which it was conceived. All of us who have written books for this series feel thoroughly committed to the idea that, while we can provide guidance to classroom teachers, it is the *teachers* who are the experts. They are aware of what specific techniques will work in their classrooms with the students they teach. Professors Costa and Lowery have provided educational practitioners with a wonderfully workable set of guidelines and suggested practices. But they have not written a cookbook for practitioners to follow blindly. Teaching for thinking will only succeed if it reflects wise choices based on a commitment to well-understood goals freely chosen by the professional who implements them.

In this spirit, the pages that follow offer teachers and administrators not only an array of good techniques but comments on both why and how they work and what they can achieve. The authors invite the reflective, informed, and deliberate choices of those reading this book. The opportunities for educational change found in these pages will, we believe, enliven and enlighten all who read them.

ROBERT J. SWARTZ AND D. N. PERKINS
SERIES EDITORS

AUTHORS' PREFACE

The ideas presented in this volume are a collection of suggested teacher behaviors, classroom organizational strategies, and instructional techniques which are the result of much research and practical experimentation. They have been tested in a variety of classrooms and school districts at a full range of ages, grades and socioeconomic levels.

Many of the original concepts resulted from early exploration and research about classroom and instructional conditions for teaching higher-level thinking and creativity. A variety of instructional strategies which had these as their goals were examined for their commonalities. As a result, several of the instructional behaviors listed in this book were described and synthesized.

We would like to thank Nobuo "Bob" Watanabe, Director of Curriculum and Instruction and Staff Development for the Contra Costa County (California) Superintendent of Schools Office for leading that effort in 1970 and to the other contributors to that early work on which so much has since been built: Bill Alkire, Sacramento County Department of Education; and Chuck Lavaroni, San Anselmo, California.

Many of the ideas here have been synthesized from the pioneering, theoretical, and research work of others. We would like to recognize them and express our appreciation to them as they have contributed greatly to our thinking, our learning, and thus, to the development of this publication:

Barry Beyer	George Mason Univeristy, Fairfax, VA
Ron Brandt	Association for Supervision and Curriculum Development, Alexandria, VA
Reuven Feuerstein	Hadassah-Wizo Canada Institute, Israel
Robin Fogarty	Illinois Renewal Institute, Shaumberg, IL
Bena Kallick	Private Consultant, Westport, CT

Francis Link	Curriculum Development Associates Washington, DC
Robert Marzano	Mid-Continent Regional Educational Laboratory, Aurora, CO
Ben Strasser	Los Angeles County Superintendent of Schools Office
J. Richard Suchman	Santa Cruz, CA (University of Illinois at Urbana, Retired)

The effectiveness of the ideas presented here should not, however, be accepted because of someone else's theories and research. You are invited to experiment with the ideas yourself; observe and record your students for their resulting behaviors; and apply these ideas not only to your classroom but also to your whole life as well. You will understand their meaning only when you have internalized them into your own personal interactions with others.

ARTHUR L. COSTA
CALIFORNIA STATE UNIVERSITY
SACRAMENTO AND

LAWRENCE LOWERY
UNIVERSITY OF CALIFORNIA
BERKELEY

INTRODUCTION

What's Basic?

Recent research, while not yet sufficient to confirm, indicates that when thinking skills become an integral part of the curriculum and instructional practice, test scores in academic areas increase (Whimbey, 1985). The ability to perform certain cognitive processes is basic to success in school subjects. Let's take outlining, for example. The ability to outline requires the skill of hierarchical thinking. If the learner is developmentally capable of hierarchical thinking, and if that cognitive function is taught prior to or along with the skill of outlining, it produces better results than if outlining were taught without that cognitive prerequisite. When reading is taught as a strategy of thinking, students increase their comprehension (Andre, 1979). When teachers take the time to teach comparative behavior, for example, students are better able to contrast, using a consistent set of attributes, the differing points of view of, e.g., the North and the South during the Civil War (Beyer, 1985).

Thinking Is for All Students

For many years thinking skills programs were intended to challenge the intellectually gifted. Some thought that any child whose IQ fell below a certain score was forever relegated to remedial or compensatory drill- and practice-type learning. However, four fundamental and refreshing concepts that underlie modern cognitive curriculum and instructional practices are gaining wide acceptance:

- *The Theory of Cognitive Modifiability* (Feuerstein, 1980),

- *The Theory of Multiple Intelligences* (Gardner, 1983),

- The faith that *Intelligence Can Be Taught* (Whimbey, 1975), and

- Sternberg's thesis that *traditional IQ scores have very little to do with success in dealing with the problems encountered in daily life* (Hammer, 1985; McKean, 1985).

These underlying theoretical concepts help us realize that *all* human beings are both retarded in certain intellectual skills and gifted in others. They provide us with the faith that *all* human beings can continue to develop their intelligent behavior throughout their lifetimes. Much research with hydrocephalic, Down's Syndrome, senile, and brain-damaged persons demonstrates that over time and with proper intervention, they can continue to make amazing growth in problem-solving abilities. Until recently, we would have given them up as hopeless.

Furthermore, and perhaps most reassuring, we are demonstrating that increasing the effectiveness of instruction produces a corresponding increase in learning. Teachers *can* grow intelligence. Teaching *is* the process of growing intelligence.

The Teacher:
The Crucial Variable in Growing Intelligence

Teachers are the ones who touch students and interact with them. They are the ones who implement educational policy and curriculum content, scope and sequence. And—most important—they are the ones who establish the educational climate and who structure learning experiences. In short, they have almost complete power over the process that takes place in the classroom. And it is my contention that process is more important than content in education (J. J. Foley, 1971).

Over the past fifteen years, much research has demonstrated that certain teacher behaviors, perceptions, and attitudes influence students' achievements, self-concepts, social relationships, and thinking abilities. More influential than tests, textbooks, curriculum, schedules, extra-curricular activities, or any other such educational factors, the teacher's power to shape students' thinking is indeed awesome. Increasingly we are finding that one of the most influential determinants of well-developed intelligence in later life is attributable to the child's verbal interaction with significant adults in early life. Parents, grandparents, older siblings, caregivers, teachers—all play an amazingly powerful role, developing in the young child those cognitive structures which will endure throughout a lifetime. While psychologists and psycholinguists have been telling educators this for many years, we never realized it so fully until it became apparent through some recent changes in our society.

We know that most thinking skills are built in the child's mind within the first few years of life—long before they come to school. Further, these skills are the result of (along with nutritional, genetic, and environmental factors) interactions with significant adults in the child's environment. With the changes in the traditional family in our culture, with an increasing number of "latchkey kids" and of children giving birth to children, and with a dramatic increase in passive television watching, there has been a corresponding decrease in the amount of verbal interaction between parents and children. Indeed, some students come to school parentally, and therefore often linguistically, deprived.

The mental development of the child is highly correlated with the complexity of language used in the home. In more affluent families, where the parents' level of education is higher, there are more questions asked and the language is more complex (Sternberg and Caruso, 1985). In poorer families, with lower levels of education, fewer questions are asked; language is more terse; fewer alternatives and choices are given about which decisions must be made; there is less need to plan ahead; and there is little need to anticipate the future. These children may come to school lacking in the experiences of planning ahead, organizing their belongings and time, comparing, choosing, and prioritizing alternatives, and/or predicting the consequences of their decisions. Thus, deprivation of language affects cognitive development.

Studies have shown that many who overcome their "disadvantaged" backgrounds succeed because of teachers and parents who served as mediators of their environment—by discussing, asking questions, modeling, and teaching. Some sociologists believe that the best way to overcome the increasing disparity between those students who profit from education and those "at-risk" students who seem resistent to learning is to train young mothers and fathers in "parenting" skills designed to develop their child's intelligence.

The Teacher as Mediator of Learning

Realizing that thinking is basic and that children's early language—and therefore certain thinking skills—may be underdeveloped, educators are finding new direction for classroom instruction: *Increasing verbal interaction.* Teaching and learning are invigorated with increased opportunities for dialogue: developing listening skills, cooperative learning, pair problem solving, thought-provoking inquiry discussions, dialogical reasoning, collaborative planning, and brainstorming. Teachers find renewed power as they stimulate students' thought processes by posing challenging questions, structuring learning activities designed to stimulate thinking, and probing for elaboration. They search for increases in diversity and creativity in student responses as they provide a safe, nonjudgmental classroom environment in which students can risk verbalizing innovative ideas. Teachers help students realize that the main purpose of their education is to develop their intellect; that they can produce their own ideas, not merely reproduce someone else's ideas.

Discussion, Not Recitation

Distinctions need to be made between two types of classroom interaction: recitation and discussion. Recitation is characterized by recurring sequences of teacher questions intended to cause students to "recite" what they already know or are coming to know through the teacher's input. The interaction is teacher centered. The teacher controls the interaction by asking the questions and reinforcing the student's responses. Discussion, on the other hand, allows group interaction in which students discuss what they don't know and put forth and consider more than one point of view on a subject. The teacher, serving as discussion leader, facilitates by creating an atmosphere of freedom, clarity, trust, and equality.

Analyses of most major programs and instructional strategies intended to enhance thinking, creativity, cooperation, and positive self-worth stress the need for this dialectic discussion strategy (Costa, 1984; Paul, 1985). Sadly, John Goodlad, in his study of over one thousand classrooms, found that little time—four to eight percent—was spent in discussion. Less than one percent of teacher talk was intended to elicit a student response (Goodlad, 1984).

In this book, the characteristics given above of classroom discussion must be kept in focus as we describe which teacher behaviors and conditions facilitate student growth in thinking skills. Our goal is to enable you, the teacher, to recognize which of your behaviors can act as tools to enhance the intellectual development of students.

Creating a Classroom Environment For Learning to Think

Over the past fifteen years, research has demonstrated the powerful influence of teaching on students' achievement, self-concepts, social relationships, and thinking abilities. Certain identifiable instructional behaviors have a direct influence on students effectively learning to think:

1. The way a teacher *structures* the classroom can enhance individual, small-group, or total-group interactions which elicit active student thinking.

2. A teacher's *directions or questions* can help students collect and recall information, process that information into meaningful relationships, apply those relationships in different or novel situations, and actively use thinking skills.

3. The way a teacher *responds* to a student's ideas or actions can help the student maintain, extend, and become aware of his/her thinking.

4. The teacher's *infusion* of opportunities for thinking into the day-to-day language and operation of classroom routines, especially when using regular curriculum materials, leads students to value good thinking.

5. Focusing on, discussing, and labeling students' *thought processes* helps them become aware of, apply, and expand their repertoire of thinking abilities and strategies.

6. The teacher's selection of *content* to be learned and the allocation of instructional time devoted to that content show students where the use of specific thinking skills are appropriate.

7. The ways by which a teacher *models* his/her own in-tellectual processes help students emulate desirable forms of thinking and intelligent behavior.

References

Andre, T. (1979). Does answering higher level questions while reading facilitate productive learning? *Review of Educational Research,* Spring, *49,* 280–318.

Beyer, B. (1985). Practical strategies for the direct teaching of thinking skills. In Costa (Ed.), *Developing Minds: A Resource Book for Teaching Thinking.* Alexandria, VA: Association for Supervision and Curriculum Development.

Costa, A. (1984). *The Enabling Behaviors.* Orangevale, CA: Search Models Unlimited.

Feuerstein, R. (1980). *Instrumental Enrichment.* Baltimore: University Park Press.

Foley, J. J. (1971). Teaching and learning in the affective domain. In J. G. Saylor and J. L. Smith (Eds.), *Removing Barriers to Humaneness in the High School.* Washington, DC: Association for Supervision and Curriculum Development.

Gardner, H. (1983). *Frames of Mind: The Theory of Multiple Intelligences.* New York: Basic Books.

Goodlad, J. (1983). *A Place Called School: Prospects for the Future.* New York: McGraw Hill.

Hammer, S. (1985). Stalking intelligence. *Science Digest,* June 6, *93,* 30–38.

McKean, K. (1985). The assault on I Q. *Discover,* October, *6,* 25–41.

Paul, R. (1984) . Critical thinking: fundamental to education for a free society. *Educational Leadership,* September, *42,* 4–16.

Sternberg, R. and Caruso, D. (1985). Practical modes of knowing. In E. Eisner (Ed.), *Learning and Teaching the Ways of Knowing: Eighty-fourth Yearbook of the National Society for the Study of Education, Part II.* Chicago: University of Chicago Press.

Swartz, R. and Perkins, D. (1989). *Teaching Thinking: Issues and Approaches.* Pacific Grove, CA: Midwest Publications.

Whimbey, A. (1985). Test results from teaching thinking. In Costa (Ed.), *Developing Minds: A Resource Book for Teaching Thinking.* Alexandria, VA: Association for Supervision and Curriculum Development.

Whimbey, A. and Whimbey, L. S. (1976). *Intelligence Can Be Taught.* New York: Bantam Books.

CHAPTER 1

STRUCTURING THE CLASSROOM FOR THINKING

Teacher A

"This ah... math lesson should enab... er... a... might get you to understand something more about some things we usually call ah... numerical progressions. Maybe before we get to the main idea of the lesson for today, you oughta, you know, review the four con... und... underlying concepts we had before. The first idea, I mean... a concept you need to review is positive integers. In fact, here's a list of the first five. Who can read them to us, uh...let's see...Mike, can you read..."

Teacher B

"This mathematics lesson will enable you to understand more about numerical progressions. Before we go to the main idea of today's lesson, I want us to review positive integers. A positive integer is any whole number greater than zero. Here on the board is a list of the first five positive integers. Mike, I'd like you to read them to us."

Which of these examples would better communicate the structure of the lesson?

∞   ∞   ∞

Structuring may be described as the several ways teachers control such classroom environmental resources as time, space, human energy, and materials. Every teacher in every classroom structures those resources. Teachers may do this consciously and unconsciously, directly and indirectly. Even the "unstructured" classroom imposes a structure to which and within which students interact.

Research in school and teaching effectiveness has repeatedly demonstrated that higher student achievement is produced in a well-structured classroom where (1) students know the objective of the lesson; (2) time is used efficiently; (3) the teacher is clear about directions; (4) the classroom environment conveys a congenial sense of order; and (5) student energies are engaged in a meaningful learning task (Kounin, 1970).

Because teacher structuring has an effect on student functioning, structuring the classroom for thinking should be conscious, deliberate, and clear. It should be based upon the desired objectives for the students. Knowing what learning tasks are to be accomplished and what type of interaction is desired, the teacher gives directions, states ground rules, describes objectives, places limits and constraints, and creates a classroom organizational pattern intended to best accomplish the desired cognitive performance of students.

In this chapter, three aspects of teacher structuring and their effects on student thinking will be described:

1. The clarity of verbal and written instructions
2. The structuring of time and energy
3. How different ways of organizing and arranging grouping and interaction patterns affects student thinking

These are three areas which call for teacher attention in developing effective techniques for the teaching of thinking skills that will enhance student learning.

1. Instructional Clarity

Teacher: "Why do you think Robert Frost repeated the last line of this verse?"

Student: (No response)

Teacher: (After a long pause) "Well, what feelings did *you* have as you read the poem?"

Student: "Why don't you just tell us the answer?"

(Wasserman, pers. com., 1978)

Students expend great energy trying to figure out the teacher's intentions. Because some students come from homes, previous teachers, or other schools where thinking skills were not valued, they often are dismayed by and resistant to the teacher's invitations to think. Such resistance and reluctance to respond should be taken as an indication that a program to develop intellectual skills is sorely needed.

Teachers must impress upon students that the goal of instruction is thinking; the responsibility for thinking is theirs; it is desirable to have more than one solution; it is commendable when they take time to plan; and an answer can be changed with additional information.

Teacher clarity is at the top of the list of effective instructional behaviors. It is consistent and positively associated with student achievement. The clarity and purpose of the teacher's directions concerning a new learning task affect student behavior. If the messages and directions presented by the teacher are confused, garbled, and unclear, then students will have a more difficult learning task. Similarly, providing too many details at one time and repeating information that the students already know increases class restlessness and the possibility for nonattentiveness (Rosenshine and Furst, 1971).

Some of the observations of instructional clarity focus on the teacher's vagueness, digressions, and redundancy. Conversely, students increase their understanding of directions when the teacher:

- frequently repeats concepts from one sentence to the next;
- says the same thing in more than one way;
- reviews prior work;
- prepares students for upcoming tasks by describing the work to be done and the means to accomplish it;
- allows time for students to think about, respond to, and synthesize what they are learning;
- involves visual and verbal examples;

- reviews difficult concepts on the chalkboard; and
- models the type of performance required in the task.

It seems imperative, therefore, that teachers' explanations be clear so that thinking is a legitimate goal of education, and that the teacher's objectives, instructional strategies, and assessment procedures are directed towards having students think. The teacher might say, for example, "Today, class, we're going to learn how to compare"; or "Today, I'm not interested in coming up with one right answer, rather I'm more interested in coming up with many divergent answers and the justification of those answers with supporting evidence."

2. Structuring Time and Energy

Research indicates that the correlation between *time* spent teaching thinking skills and student achievement in basic skills (as measured at certain grade levels by standardized tests) parallels achievement in other areas of learning (Borg, 1980).

If thinking is to be a highly valued goal in our schools, substantial time must be allocated for student and teacher participation. The intellect, much like the musculature, needs constant exercise over extended periods of time to perform with efficiency, synergism, and fluid grace.

But how much time is enough time? This can only be answered in terms of the needs of a particular population of students. A survey of the most popular curricula and programs for teaching thinking suggests that, using carefully designed materials and well-planned and executed lessons, at least two to three hours per week is needed to permanently affect students' cognitive abilities. Furthermore, it seems this intensity needs to be maintained for a period of at least two years for mastery and durable installation of these mental functions.

With an educational organization that typically tracks students in one-year or semester segments and fifty-five-minute periods, it may prove difficult to provide instructional continuity for this duration. Furthermore, emphasis on thinking cannot be viewed by the student as an isolated event occurring only when an itinerant teacher arrives, or as a period on Thursday from 2:00 to 2:53 labeled "thinking time." Rather, students must repeatedly receive instruction in cognitive skills and encounter situations throughout the school day that require thinking. This needs to take place across academic content areas and over extended periods of time. When this happens, there is greater possibility for transference, generalization, and application of a cognitive skill (Sternberg and Wagner, 1982). For some schools, this may require a revision of curriculum goals, school organization, allocation of time, and assessment procedures.

Structuring time alone, however, is inadequate. Consideration must also be given to the quality of the task during that time: how engaged are students' *energies* during that time. According to Piaget's constructivist theory, all knowledge arises—or is constructed—from interactions between learners and their environment. That is, to the extent that teachers mediate the interaction of pupils with instructional materials and with the content of the lesson, those skills are likely to be learned. *Active* learning has a positive effect on students' development of decision-making/ problem-solving skills, as well as on their attitudes toward school, teachers, the content to be learned, and learning itself.

3. Organizing the Classroom for Thinking

Teachers can organize their classrooms in a variety of ways to facilitate students becoming actively—not passively—involved in thinking. This might include teacher led, Socratic-type discussions, individual manipulations, and cooperative small-group or total-group investigations. These features of classroom organizations are prime factors in creating the kind of classroom atmosphere for thinking referred to in the first volume of this series (Swartz and Perkins, 1988).

Of all the various patterns of classroom organization that a teacher might use, some achieve better results than others for certain students, at certain grade levels, and for certain goals of instruction. Below are descriptions of several classroom organizational patterns with discussions of their usefulness in teaching thinking.

Discussions are characterized by teacher- or student-led interactions in which some topic, question, problem, or issue is raised for consideration. Students offer ideas, solutions, or points of view, while other students listen, consider alternatives, evaluate ideas, and offer evidence to support their suggestions. The teacher facilitates by asking questions, clarifying, paraphrasing, recording ideas on the board or chart paper, calling on students, and regulating the pace of the interaction. It has been found that students learn more in a question-and-answer discussion strategy. Greater gains are made when teachers spend time discussing, explaining, asking higher-level questions, and stimulating cognitive processes than when students are working quietly or individually. This is probably due to the students' role in language production, listening, and intellectual stimulation.

Group work is characterized by subdivision of the class into work groups or committees. Objectives for the group may be assigned, roles in the group (such as chairperson, recorder, process observer, etc.) may be clarified, and standards for harmonious group work may be set. While the groups are working, the teacher monitors their progress. This organizational pattern has great advantages for developing thinking skills. The Johnsons found that when students work cooperatively in groups, increased reasoning strategies and greater critical thinking competencies result than in competitive or individualistic settings (Johnson and Johnson, 1983).

Individual work is characterized by students working by themselves. All students could be doing the same task or each student could be performing a different task. They would not, however, be interacting with each other or with the teacher. Individual work may be ineffective if it is not carefully monitored by the teacher. Students may be "off-task" more and a greater number of errors may go uncorrected when the teacher does not constantly monitor individual student's learning.

The lecture method has long been found wanting in terms of student learning. Early studies have shown that there are vast individual differences in the amounts of learning experienced by students in a lecture situation (Jones, 1923). Furthermore, lecture content is often forgotten. Ebbinhous (1913) found that the curve of retention dropped from about sixty percent on immediate recall after the lecture to about twenty percent after eight weeks.

Providing for individual differences

Different students need different classroom organizational patterns. Some students learn best individually; some learn best in groups. There are students who learn best when an adult is present to constantly encourage and reinforce them; others have difficulty learning when another person is nearby. Some students need noise, others need quiet; some need bright light, some need subdued light; some need formal settings, others need informal situations; some need to move, others need to be stationary.

Some students need a great deal of structure and others need minimal structure. Less able students do better in highly structured learning situations where direct help is generous while more able students profit from less structured situations (Dunn and Dunn, 1978).

Administrators and teachers will want to provide for a variety of organizational patterns in the classroom to better meet the individual learning needs of students as they accomplish a variety of learning objectives. If teachers have only one way of organizing the classroom for instruction, it may be appropriate for only a small number of students. If, however, the teacher can call upon a repertoire of organizational patterns, it may reach a wider range of students' interests, abilities, styles, and objectives.

Structuring for thinking

What kind of classroom structure, then, produces the greatest achievement in thinking skills and strategies? Thomas states:

> Where the locus of control over learning-related behaviors is entirely vested in the teacher, where maximum structure is provided for carrying out learning activities, and where the motivation to perform is provided for through external rewards, praise, and/or fear of reprisal, there is little latitude or opportunity for students to develop a sense of agency and, subsequently, to become proficient in using learning strategies.... What may be required is an instructional procedure replete with tasks for which strategies have some payoff and perhaps a deliberate attempt to teach and/or allow for the discovery of varieties of cognitive strategies appropriate to these tasks (Thomas, 1980, 236).

In support of Thomas' statement above, further research by McKnight and Waxman (1986) indicates that direct instruction, where the teacher is making most of the decisions about the content the student is learning, may be an inhibitor to students' higher-level and creative thinking.

What most authorities in curriculum and instruction promote, and what the authors above support with research, is that when higher-level thinking, creativity, and problem solving are the objectives, students must be in a classroom climate where they are in the decision-making role; they decide on strategies to solve problems; they determine the correctness or incorrectness of an answer based upon data they produced and validated; and they are involved in setting their own goals and means of assessing accomplishment of those goals.

Furthermore, the reward system in such a classroom should be intrinsic to the task rather than extrinsic, based upon the teacher's responses. It should be derived from internal motivation to learn—intellectual curiosity about phenomena; a striving for craftsmanship and accuracy; a desire to be a responsible, productive and interdependent member of a community of scholars; and a desire to emulate significant, respected others.

Teachers who value internal rather than external rewards, engage students in structuring their own learning, realize human variability in learning, and can teach toward multiple goals will use a repertoire of classroom organizational patterns. Classrooms organized for thinking will be characterized by:

>*Individual students* working alone, engaged in a task requiring one or more cognitive skills, e.g., comparing, classifying, sorting, evaluating, etc. During individual work, teachers will be monitoring their progress and mediating their experiences.

>*Groups* will be working *cooperatively* on collaborative problem-solving tasks: planning strategies for group projects; contributing data and ideas to the progress of the project; identifying what information still needs to be gathered and devising strategies to generate that information; and evaluating individual and group social skills. During group work, teachers will be monitoring their progress, assessing growth in social and cognitive abilities, and mediating both the intellectual skills required of the task *and* the cooperative group skills.

>At other times *the total group* will be engaged in listening to presentations by and interacting with the teacher, resource people, and media. Socratic discussions, dialectical reasoning, and/or class meetings (circle of knowledge) will also be employed when the teacher or a student poses a dilemma, states a problem, or notes a discrepancy. Thereby, all students may participate in debating, considering alternative points of view, and selecting and evaluating an appropriate resolution.

To learn to think, students must engage in, discuss, and come to value thinking. John Goodlad in his book *A Place Called School* reports that less than one percent of teacher talk invited a student response (Goodlad, 1983). As schools come to value thinking, this teacher behavior will be replaced with engaging students in individual interaction, both in small groups and in total groups, with problem-solving and creative activities designed and evaluated by students themselves.

References

Borge, W. R. (1980). Time and school learning. In C. Denham and A. Lieberman (Eds.), *Time to Learn,* Washington, DC: National Institute of Education, 43-72.

Dunn, R. and Dunn, K. (1978). *Teaching Students through Their Individual Learning Styles.* Reston, VA: Reston Publishing Co.

Ebbinhous, H. (1913). *Memory.* A. Henry (Trans.), New York: Teachers College, Columbia University.

Goodlad, J. (1983). *A Place Called School: Prospects for the Future.* New York: McGraw Hill.

Johnson, R. and Johnson, D. and others. (1984). *Circles of Learning: Cooperation in the Classroom.* Alexandria: VA, Association for Supervision and Curriculum Development.

Jones, H. E. (1923). Experimental studies of college teaching. *Archives of Psychology.* November, *68,* entire issue.

Knight, S. and Waxman, H. (1987). Analyzing the relationship between teachers' classroom behaviors and students' rational thinking skills. Paper presented at the third international conference on thinking. Honolulu.

Kounin, J. S. (1970). *Discipline and Group Management in Classrooms.* New York: Holt, Rinehart and Winston.

Rosenshine, B. and Furst, N. (1971). Current and future research on teacher performance criteria. In B. Smith (Ed.), *Research on Teacher Education: A Symposium.* Englewood Cliffs, NJ: Prentice Hall.

Sternberg, R. and Wagner, R. (1982). *Understanding intelligence: what's in it for education?* Paper submitted to the National Commission on Excellence in Education.

Swartz, R. and Perkins, D. (1989). *Teaching Thinking: Issues and Approaches.* Pacific Grove, CA: Midwest Publications.

Thomas, J. (1980). Agency and achievement: self-management and self-regard. *Review of Educational Research,* Summer, *50,* 213-240.

Wasserman, Selma. Conversation with author, A.S.C.D. conference, 1978, in Anaheim, CA.

CHAPTER 2

TEACHER-INITIATED QUESTIONS AND DIRECTIONS THAT ELICIT THINKING AND LEARNING

Teacher:	"What were the names of the children in the story?"
Student A:	"Tom, Kevin, and Sarah."
Teacher:	"Good. In what country did they live?"
Student B:	"Germany."
Teacher:	"Yes, good. Where did Tom's parents work?"
Student C:	"On the air force base."
Teacher:	"Very good."

In the above sample of classroom interaction, what kind of thinking is occurring? How much language are the students producing? How complex is that language? Compare this with the sample below:

Teacher:	"Why do you think this American family might be living in Germany?"
Student A:	"One reason could be that they've been transferred there. I have a friend whose father works for an aircraft company and they moved to Germany."
Teacher:	"That's possible. Other ideas?"
Student B:	"Maybe they're on vacation."
Teacher:	"Could be. What makes you think so?"

Student B: "Well, there's a riverboat in the picture; and it looks like summer. I don't think they live there; they're just visiting."

Student C: "The man is wearing a uniform. I think they're living on an air force base in Germany—Frankfurt, I think, is a place where we have an air force base. My dad was stationed in Germany when he was in the air force."

∞   ∞   ∞

Early in life, children learn to listen and respond to language. From questions and other statements that parents pose, youngsters derive cues for what is expected of them. When the children enter school, they find that teachers, too, guide expectancies through questions and directions.

Teachers use questions to elicit certain cognitive objectives or thinking skills. Embedded in these questions and in statements are cues for the cognitive task or behavior that the student is to carry out.

There is a relationship between the type of thinking inherent in the teacher's verbal behavior and the type of thinking students use in response. For example, a teacher may pose a question or statement using syntax that signals that a specific answer is wanted: "When did Columbus first come to the Western Hemisphere?" The teacher may also choose syntax to signal divergent thought: "How do you think the United States might have developed differently had the early explorers come across the Pacific rather than the Atlantic Ocean?" Correlations have been found between the syntax of the teacher's questions and the syntax of the student's response. Furthermore, teachers whose questions frequently require divergent thinking elicit more divergent thinking on the part of students than teachers who use more cognitive memory questions. Higher scores on tests of critical thinking and on standardized achievement tests result when teachers use a range of convergent and divergent thinking questions.

A Model of Thinking

Realizing that teachers can cause the students to think by carefully designing the syntax of questions and statements, let us now focus on a model of thinking. The model below will serve as a basis for the composition of questions. By composing questions and statements with certain syntactical arrangements, teachers can cause the student to perform the intellectual functions represented in this model.

Model of Thinking

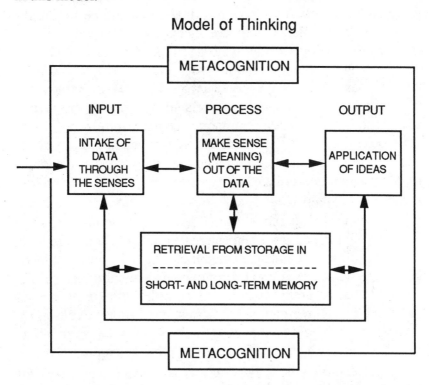

Most authors distinguish three to five basic thought clusters (Smith and Tyler, 1945):

- *Input* of data through the senses;
- *Retrieval* of the information from short- and long-term memory storage;

- *Processing* of that data through various thinking structures into meaningful relationships by comparing or relating it with information in short- and long-term memory;

- *Output* or application of those relationships to new or novel situations; and

- *Metacognition*—thinking about our own thinking.

Thinking is the internal processing of external stimuli received through the senses. If the new information should be stored, the brain attempts to match, compare, categorize, and pattern it with similar information already in storage. This process is done very quickly in an apparently random order, either at the conscious or unconscious level. Thus, every event a person experiences causes the brain to call up meaningful, related information from storage—whether the event is commonplace or a carefully developed classroom learning experience. The more meaningful, relevant, and complex the experience, the more actively the brain attempts to integrate and assimilate it into its existing storehouse of programs and structures.

According to this model of intellectual functioning, the most complex thinking occurs when external stimuli challenge the brain to (1) draw upon the greatest amount of data or structures already in storage; (2) expand an already existing structure; and (3) develop new structures. Many of the complex thinking activities identified in volume one of this series, e.g., informal reasoning, involve these three ingredients. If thinking skills are taught effectively, students who think effectively will be the product.

A problem may be defined as any stimulus or challenge, the response to which is not readily apparent. If there is a ready match between what is perceived by the senses and what is in an existing structure or program already in storage, no problem exists. Piaget calls this *assimilation*. If, however, the new information cannot be explained or resolved with knowledge in short- or long-term memory, the information must be processed, action taken to gather more information to resolve the discrepancy, and the ultimate resolution evaluated for its "fit" with reality. Piaget refers to this as *accommodation*. Our brains seem to dislike disequilibrium and constantly strive to satisfy and resolve discrepancies perceived in the environment.

The model of thinking illustrated above provides only a simple schematic representation of intellectual functioning. By its use we do not mean to imply that such complexities as motivation, affect, and attitude are not important in effective thinking. Indeed they are, and we shall discuss their role in chapter 7. This model enables us to help students develop and improve their thinking.

Inviting Student Thinking

Using a model of how the mind thinks and learns, the teacher can intelligently structure questions and statements to engage the student in particular activities that enhance and improve thinking.

Below are some examples a teacher might use to cause the students to use their senses; recall from memory; process the ideas; use or apply the knowledge in some action; and transfer or evaluate those relationships in new or hypothetical situations.

1. Gathering information (INPUT)

To cause the student to *input* data, questions can be designed to activate the senses to gather data that the student can then process. There are several thinking processes included at the *input* level of thinking.

Some verbs that may serve as predicates in statements of desired behavior are:

seeing	viewing	hearing
listening	tasting	feeling
touching	smelling	sniffing

Consonant with some of the examples in the first volume in this series, we can distinguish uses of the skills involved in this input stage. They are related to direct perception and to the indirect intake of information through communication with other people or from written sources of information (Swartz and Perkins, 1989).

Examples of questions or statements designed to elicit these cognitive objectives might be:

Question/Statement	Desired Cognitive Behavior
"What do you see in the box?"	Seeing
"How does it taste?"	Tasting
"What do you hear in the shell?"	Listening
"Let's watch the film.	Viewing

2. Recalling information from short- and long-term memory (RETRIEVING)

Questions and statements can be designed to draw from the student the concepts, information, feelings, or experiences acquired in the past and stored in long- or short-term memory. Some helpful verbs might be:

describing	listing	identifying
recalling	defining	reciting
completing	counting	naming

Examples of questions or statements designed to elicit these cognitive objectives might be:

Question/Statement	Desired Cognitive Behavior
"Name the states which bound California."	Naming
"What do you need from the store?"	Listing
"Which words in this list are rhyming words?"	Identifying
"How many coins are in the stack?"	Counting

Question/Statement	Desired Cognitive Behavior
"The Eskimos' houses were made of ice blocks and are called...what?"	Completing
"List the first four numbers in a set of positive integers."	Listing
"What was your score on the algebra test?"	Recalling

3. Making sense out of the information gathered (PROCESSING)

Students can be led to process data gathered through the senses and retrieved from long- and short-term memory. This is best accomplished by designing questions and statements to facilitate drawing cause-and-effect relationships, synthesizing, analyzing, summarizing, and comparing content, or classifying the data the student has acquired or observed. Below are verbs that can serve as predicates for such questions and statements, if the goal is to process data into meaningful relationships.

synthesizing	analyzing	categorizing
explaining	classifying	comparing
contrasting	grouping	relating
experimenting	organizing	distinguishing
sequencing	summarizing	stating causality
	making analogies	

Below are examples of questions designed to elicit these cognitive objectives:

Question/Statement	Desired Cognitive Behavior
"Compare the strength of steel to the strength of copper."......................	Comparing
"Why did Columbus believe he could get to the East by sailing west?"	Explaining
"What do you think caused the liquid to turn blue?"............................	Stating causality
"What other machines can you think of that work on the same principle as this one?".........................	Making analogies
"How can you arrange the blocks to give a crowded feeling?"	Organizing
"How are pine needles different from redwood needles?"............................	Contrasting
"How does the formula for finding the volume of a cone compare with the formula for the volume of a pyramid?"	Comparing
"Arrange the following elements of a set in ascending order: 13/4, 3/2, 5/6, 32/5."	Sequencing

4. Applying and evaluating actions in novel situations (OUTPUT)

To lead the student beyond the concept or principle he/she has developed to a novel or hypothetical situation, the teacher needs to use questions and statements similar to those below. Application invites the student to think creatively and hypothetically, use imagination, expose or apply a value system, or make a critical judgment. It is in this group that most of the complex thinking activities discussed in volume one in this series are located. Also listed below are cognitive behaviors designed to lead to OUTPUT.

applying a principle	imagining	planning
evaluating	judging	predicting
extrapolating	creating	forecasting
inferring	hypothesizing	speculating
generalizing	model building	designing

Examples of questions designed to elicit these cognitive objectives are:

Question/Statement	Desired Cognitive Behavior
"If our population continues to grow as it has been, what will life be like in the twenty-first century?"	Speculating
"What can you say about all countries' economies that are dependent upon only one crop?"	Generalizing
"What would be the fairest solution to this problem?"	Evaluating
"From what we have learned, which painting is the best example of modern art?"	Judging
"What do you think might happen if we placed the salt-water fish in the fresh-water aquarium?"	Hypothesizing
"From our experiments with food coloring in different water temperatures, what can you infer about the movement of molecules?"	Inferring

5. Thinking about our own thinking (METACOGNITION)

(This will take some special explanation beyond the scope of this chapter and will be discussed in chapter 5.)

Teachers have an awesome power. Through the careful and selective use of questions and statements, they can elicit, invite, and cause students to perform these cognitive behaviors. It is hypothesized that over time, as a result of the use of such questions, students will:

- decode the teacher's verbal syntax of questions and other statements and respond with corresponding cognitive processes;

- experience and thus exercise these cognitive processes;

- become aware of these cognitive processes;

- apply these cognitive processes beyond the classroom;

- value teachers', parents', and others' invitations to think;

- increase their own inclination and desire to ask a range of questions.

Further Readings on Teacher Questions And Student Cognition

Andre, T. (1979). Does answering higher level questions while reading facilitate productive learning? *Review of Educational Research,* Spring, *49,* 280-318.

Bloom, B. et al. (1956). *Taxonomy of Educational Objectives Handbook I: Cognitive Domain.* New York: David McKay Co.

Carin, A. and Sund, R. (1971). *Developing Questioning Technique: A Self-Concept Approach.* Columbus: Charles E. Merrill Co.

Crump, C. (1970). Teachers, questions and cognition. *Educational Leadership,* April, 657-660.

Costa, A. (1985). Teacher behaviors that enable student thinking. In A. Costa (Ed.), *Developing Minds: A Resource Book for Teaching Thinking.* Alexandria, VA: Association for Supervision and Curriculum Development.

———— (1986). *The Enabling Behaviors.* Orangevale, CA: Search Models Unlimited.

Dillon, J. (1984). Research on questioning and discussion. *Educational Leadership,* November, *42.*

Egan, K. (1975). How to ask questions to promote higher level thinking. *Peabody Journal of Education,* April.

Gall, M. (1970). The use of questions in teaching. *Review of Educational Research,* December, *40,* 207-220.

Hunkins, F. (1972). *Questioning Strategies and Techniques.* Rockleigh, NJ: Allyn Bacon.

Lowery, L., and Marshall, H. (1980). *Learning More about Learning: Teacher Initiated Statements and Questions.* Berkeley: University of California.

Saunders, N. (1966). *Classroom Questions: What Kinds?* New York: Harper and Row.

Servey, R. (1974). *Teacher Talk: The Knack of Asking Questions.* Belmont, CA: Fearon Publishers.

Wease, H. (1976). Questioning: the genius of teaching and
    learning. *High School Journal,* March.
Winne, P. (1979). Experiments relating teachers' use of higher
    cognitive questions to student achievement.
    Review of Educational Research, Winter, *49,* 13-50.

CHAPTER 3

TEACHER RESPONSE BEHAVIORS THAT SUPPORT AND EXTEND THINKING AND LEARNING

Teacher:	"How do you think our country would have developed differently had the early explorers landed on the West Coast and moved east across our country rather than landing on the East Coast and moving west across our country—an eastward movement rather than a westward movement?"
Student A:	"Our laws would be different."
Teacher:	"No."
Student B:	"Our language might be different."
Teacher:	"No."
Student C:	"It would have taken longer to populate our country because the mountains and deserts would have kept the settlers on the West Coast longer."
Teacher:	"Yes, good for you."

∞   ∞   ∞

In the above example, how has the teacher's response to students' ideas inhibited or extended students' thinking? How would you have felt if your idea were discredited, put down, or ignored? How would you feel toward other students whose ideas were praised and valued while yours were criticized?

The teacher's manner of responding to students greatly influences them. Lowery and Marshall (1979) found that this influence is greater than the teacher's questioning or directions. Students are constantly anticipating how their teacher will respond to their actions. It has also been found that the teacher's responses have a great influence on the development of students' self-concepts, their attitudes toward learning, their achievements, and their classroom rapport.

What Are Teacher Response Behaviors?

Response behaviors may be categorized according to the effect those behaviors have on students: those that tend to terminate or close down thinking; and those that maintain, open up, or extend thinking. There are six behaviors that can be classified under these two categories:

> *Terminal or closed responses*
>> >>Criticizing (and other put-downs)
>> >>Praising
>
> *Open or extending responses*
>> >>Using silence (wait time)
>> >>Accepting—passively, actively, or empathetically
>> >>Clarifying—of both concept and process
>> >>Providing information

Much research accumulated over several years supports the theory that students benefit when teachers use these behaviors in the manner suggested here. Descriptions and explanations of each behavior and the research supporting its use are presented on the following pages.

TERMINAL OR CLOSED RESPONSES

>>   *Criticizing (and other-put downs)*

Criticism may be defined as a negative value judgment. When a teacher responds to a student's ideas or actions with such negative words as "poor," "incorrect," or "wrong," the response tends to signal inadequacy or disapproval and terminates the student's thinking about the task. Negative responses can sometimes be subtle, such as "You're *almost* right," or "Who has a *better* answer?" or "You're getting *close*." Sometimes negative responses take the form of ridicule: "What a dumb idea," or "You're not good enough."

On some occasions teachers may employ sarcastic responses or negative inflections: "Who would want to help you when you act *that* way?" or "Where on earth did you get *that* idea?" or "Now that Mary is finished, who will show us the way it *should* be done?"

The use of criticism is *not* an appropriate response since it leaves the student with feelings of failure and cognitive inadequacy and contributes to a poor self-concept. It does not encourage or enhance thinking.

Abundant research has found that the use of criticism is not helpful in promoting learning (Soar, 1972). When teachers respond to students with criticism, the result is negative pupil attitudes and lower pupil achievement.

>> *Praising*

Praise, the opposite of criticism, employs positive value judgments, such as "good," "excellent," and "great." Below are some examples of teacher responses that use praise:

"That was a very *good* answer, Linda."

"Your painting is *excellent*."

"You're such a *fine* boy today, Leo."

"Yours was the *best* example that anybody gave."

Surprisingly, while many teachers advocate the use of praise in attempts to reinforce behaviors and to build self-worth, the research on praise indicates that more often its effect is negative. Praise builds conformity. It makes students depend on *others* for their worth rather than upon *themselves*.

Some teachers use praise so often and indiscriminately that it becomes a meaningless response, and students derive little benefit from it. Praise is, however, appropriate under certain conditions. Learning to recognize and use praise sparingly and judiciously— only in these circumstances, with only these students, and for only these objectives for which it is suitable—is a desirable teacher goal. It is also desirable that teachers replace praising with an enlarged repertoire of response behaviors that research indicates are more conducive to developing students' thinking skills.

Circumstances where praise is warranted

Praising is helpful with only certain students and for certain tasks. Below are three circumstances in which praise does seem warranted.

With reluctant, unmotivated, dependent learners. Some students are difficult to motivate. They are highly dependent upon the teacher for reinforcement and need constant reminders to stay on task. These are often students who, when given an assignment, soon lose interest, have a limited attention span, and who quickly seek redirection. While praise often benefits this type of learner, the teacher should set the goal for them of replacing external reinforcement with internal motivation. For this, the amount and frequency of teacher praise must gradually be reduced, to be replaced with the satisfaction he/she derives from solving intriguing problems, the accuracy and craftsmanship of tasks completed, and the responsibility for contributing to group accomplishment. Thus, with this type of learner, the teacher must consciously withdraw praise over time (fading). Often, when a new or difficult learning is begun, praise will need to be used again briefly until the student has a feeling of confidence and mastery.

With lower grade-level students. Kohlberg has described a sequence through which students grow in their understanding of social justice and moral reasoning. During early stages, children "understand" right and wrong because of the "rewards and punishments" given by adults and others in authority. These rewards and punishments are the consequences of their behavior. In later life, students can understand the consequences of their behavior because of their effect on others or because they understand what is "morally ethical" behavior.

While students are still in the early stages of moral development, praise and rewards may be appropriate. These stages are not necessarily determined by chronological maturity, but rather by observation of students' behavior in situations requiring social decision making and by analyzing discussions with children about appropriate behavior in varying problem situations. Higher-level, more autonomous and appropriate, kind and just behaviors will develop in students if they are involved in decisions and problem situations that require making a choice of behaviors. It is helpful if their behaviors are discussed and analyzed with them, and if significant adults in their environment model those more appropriate social behaviors.

While praise may seem to be more appropriate with young, morally immature students, we want to help them progress beyond that stage. Teachers, therefore, must soon abolish praising and replace it with the type of internal motivation system which is consistent with the higher stages of moral development.

Low-level cognitive tasks. Input questions, as mentioned earlier, are used so students confirm or produce an answer from memory or from sensory observations. It is probable that the answer the student gives is predictable and therefore "correct." The teacher's response to the student's answer to an input question may involve praise. For example:

Teacher: "What is the largest city in California?"

Student: "San Francisco?"

Teacher: "No, Jane, not San Francisco."

Student: "Los Angeles?"

Teacher: "Yes, Bill, that's correct. Los Angeles is the largest."

Some guidelines for using praise

If praise is used, there are some guidelines that can help students decrease their dependence on it:

Giving the criteria or rationale for the value judgment. If praise is given, it is important that the criteria for it be described. What makes an act "good" or "excellent" must be communicated along with the praise. Thereby, the student understands the reason or criteria that make the act acceptable so that the performance can be repeated.

Helping students analyze their own answers:

Teacher: "Jane says San Francisco is the largest city in California. Bill says Los Angeles is the largest. Would each of you please tell us what is the population of the two cities? One way to find out is to compare our data."

In the previous paragraphs, we have described the strengths and limitations of the use of the terminal response behaviors, criticizing and praising. The limited conditions governing the use of praise or positive value judgments have been described. It is intended that the use of these terminal behaviors be *decreased* and that alternative response behaviors that have a more instructive effect on students' cognitive development be increased. These alternatives will be discussed later in this chapter.

Rewards and praise

Most teachers enjoy rewarding and praising their students. Brophy (1981), however, found that the one person in the classroom for whom praise has the most beneficial effect is, indeed, the teacher. For this reason, it is understandable that research studies showing the detrimental effects of rewards are met with resistance.

In a few situations, rewards and praise may be warranted, but the research indicates that there are other instructional situations in which it is *not*. The judicious use of praise seems to depend upon discriminating (1) what kind of learners need it and (2) which instructional goals and objectives warrant it.

First, such learning variables as interest, motivation, achievement, perseverance, and internal locus of control are all adversely affected when the teacher uses praise and rewards. When teachers reduce verbal rewarding, children demand less time for "showing and telling." Students then increase comparison and discussion leading to experimentation. Speculation also increases. When praise and rewards are given, they tend to inhibit experimentation (Rowe, 1974).

Second, research shows that high levels of praise affect the sociometrics of the classroom. Students receiving praise from the teacher are more often selected by their classmates as those most desired to be and work with. In those classrooms where praise was withheld, a more diffused sociometric pattern resulted; i.e., greater numbers of students, rather than a few "stars," were selected workmates (Daily, 1970).

Third, much teacher praise is associated with lower pupil nonverbal creativity. Reinforcement through the use of such comments as "uh-huh" and "okay" was positively related to some achievement scores, while frequent use of stronger praise was not (Wallen and Wodtke, 1963).

While teachers may have good intentions when using praise or rewards, how the student interprets these actions is more important in determzining whether they will have their intended effect. Teachers must be sensitive to the individual student's interpretation of rewards and praise and will, therefore, choose to praise or reward according to the timing, circumstances, and type of reward and praise to be given.

What type of learner needs praise? If students are already motivated when they are involved in the desired behaviors, rewards can be counterproductive. Rather than reinforcing the enthusiasm that is present and increasing the student's motivation, the additional praise may actually reduce them.

Some students, unfortunately, lack motivation. Praise is not, however, usually effective in this situation. Teachers using rewards and praise as motivators actually increase the students' dependency on others. Instead, students need to find learning inherently satisfying, or to acquire or exercise skills which they value themselves (Lepper and Greene, 1978).

Praise can be effective, however, with younger children. In kindergarten through second or even third grades, most children are compliant and oriented toward conforming to and pleasing their teachers. They are learning classroom and school rules, procedures, and routines, as well as how to function as members of a group. Praise and rewards seem appropriate in the socialization process at this early grade level.

As children mature (grades two, three, and beyond), they have learned what they need to know about school and classroom routines and procedures, and less and less time needs to be spent on such conforming behavior. While a first-grade boy might be delighted when his teacher pointed out his behavior, the same boy in the fifth grade would be horrified if the teacher said, "I like the way John is sitting nice and tall, ready to begin work."

Which instructional objectives warrant praise? Flanders (1970) stated

> The pupil growth index which involves memory, a relatively low level cognitive task, can tolerate lower levels of teacher indirectness....yet higher levels of cognitive reasoning are associated with more indirect...teacher influence pattern. Creativity appears to flourish most with the most indirect patterns.

Further refinements need to be made in respect to teacher praise. While rewards may inhibit creativity and personal satisfaction, especially in older students, praise may be effective when it is a question of the learning product.

The learning *process* differs from the learning *product*. Because of this, rewards for tasks already learned (the *product*) are not detrimental because the *process* of learning has already occurred, and the focus is now on learner production of what he or she already knows.

In contrast, the *process* of learning may be detrimentally affected by rewards. This is not the case in student performance on routine, familiar procedures. (In fact, when students do not particularly like assignments that are repetitious and designed to give them practice, rewards seem to enhance their performance.) However, as soon as students engage in more creative thinking, the process is inhibited by praise.

It is important that teachers not rely on rewards and praise to motivate students. These techniques may be effective with young students and when it is a question of the learning product or of routine, familiar procedures. However, rewards have a detrimental effect on older students' performance on tasks requiring higher-level problem solving. The performance of learning new tasks, skills, and processes requires cognitive risks and exploration which are inhibited by praise and promised reward.

OPEN OR EXTENDING RESPONSES

>> *Using silence (wait time)*

Many teachers wait only one or two seconds after having asked a question before they call on another student, ask another question, or give the answer to the question themselves. They feel that unless someone is talking, no one is learning. Sometimes periods of silence may seem interminably long. If, however, students are to be given opportunities to do their own thinking, their own reflecting, their own problem solving and determining an answer's appropriateness, then teachers need to be comfortable in allowing these periods of silence to occur.

If the teacher waits after asking a question or after a student gives an answer, there are observable differences in the classroom behaviors of students. If the teacher waits only a short time—one or two seconds—then short, one-word type student responses will result. On the other hand, if the teacher waits for longer periods, the students tend to respond in whole sentences and complete thoughts. There is a perceptible increase in the creativity of the response as shown by greater use of descriptive and modifying words. There is also increased speculativeness in the students' thinking. Research has shown that the student-to-student interaction is greater, the number of questions students ask increases, and previously shy students begin to contribute (Rowe, 1974).

Teachers communicate their expectations through the use of silence. When the teacher asks a question and then waits for a student's answer, it demonstrates that the teacher not only expects an answer but also has faith in the student's ability to answer, given enough time. If the teacher asks a question and then waits only a short time, gives the answer or calls on another student, gives a hint, or seeks help from another student, it suggests that the student is incompetent to answer or even to offer an answer or reason for him/herself.

When the teacher waits after the student gives an answer, the student continues thinking about the task or question. When a teacher waits after the student asks a question, it models for the student thoughtfulness, reflectiveness, and restraint of impulsivity—valued traits of effective thinkers.

>> *Accepting responses*

Teachers who are nonevaluative and nonjudgmental accept what students do. When they accept, they give no clues through posture, gesture, or word whether a student's idea, behavior, or feeling is good or bad, better or worse, right or wrong. In response to a student's idea or action, acceptance of it provides a psychologically safe climate where the student can take risks, is entrusted with the responsibility of making decisions for himself, and can explore the consequences of his own actions. Acceptance provides conditions in which students are encouraged to examine and compare their own data, values, ideas, criteria, and feelings with those of others as well as those of the teacher. Even though these values and feelings may differ from those of the teacher, teachers can still accept these differences because they know that only the student is able to modify them for thinking.

While teachers may respond by accepting in different ways, three types of accepting responses are given here: (1) passive acceptance, (2) active acceptance and (3) empathetic acceptance.

Passive acceptance is a teacher response that simply receives and acknowledges, without value judgments, what the student says. It communicates that the student's ideas have been heard. Examples of this type of response are:

"Um-hmm," "That's one possibility," "Could be," or "I understand" (passive, verbal accepting responses).

Nodding or recording without change the student's statement on the chalkboard (passive, nonverbal accepting responses).

Active acceptance is a teacher response that reflects what the student says or does by rephrasing, paraphrasing, recasting, translating, or summarizing. Teachers use this response when they want to extend, build upon, compare, or give an example based upon what the student has said. While the teacher may use different words from the student, the teacher strives to maintain the intent and accurate meaning of the student's idea.

Active acceptance is more meaningful than passive acceptance because the teacher demonstrates not only that the student's message has been received but also that it is understood.

Drawing on many supportive studies, Flanders (1960) stated in this regard:

> "The percentage of teacher statements that make use of ideas and opinions previously expressed by pupils is directly related to average class scores on attitude scales of teacher attractiveness, liking the class, etc., as well as average achievement scores adjusted for initial ability. Attitude as well as language usage, social studies skills, arithmetic computation, and problem solving were correlated with the teacher behaviors which used or extended students' ideas. Achievement was high in classrooms where these behaviors were used by the teacher."

Examples of this type of response are:

"Your explanation is that if the heat were increased, the molecule would move faster and therefore disperse the food coloring faster."

"I understand. Your idea is that we all write our legislators rather than send one letter from the group."

"Juan's idea is that the leaves could be classified according to their shapes, while Sarah's way is to group them by size."

"Our arranging our rock collection according to several different classification systems is an example of your idea."

Empathetic acceptance is a response that accepts feelings as well as content. Teachers respond this way when they want to accept a student's feelings, emotions, or behaviors. Often teachers show empathy when they express similar feelings based upon their own experiences. Such responses communicate that the teacher not only "hears" the student's idea but also the emotions underlying the idea. Empathic acceptance does *not* mean that the teacher condones acts of aggression or destructive behavior. Some examples of this type of response are:

"I can see why you're confused. Those directions are unclear to me, too."

"You're frustrated because you didn't get a chance to share your idea. We all must take turns, and that requires patience. It's hard to wait when you want to share."

The student enters the room and slams a math workbook on the desk. The teacher responds empathetically to this behavior by saying, "Something must be upsetting you today. Did you have difficulty with that assignment?"

>> *Clarifying*

Clarifying is similar to accepting in that both behaviors reflect the teacher's concern for fully understanding the student's idea. While active acceptance demonstrates that the teacher *does* understand, the need to clarify shows that the teacher *does not* understand what the student is saying and therefore, is seeking more information.

When a student uses some terminology, expresses a concept or idea, or asks a question the teacher does not understand, the teacher may wish to *clarify* both the *content* of that idea and/or the *process* by which that idea was derived. Teachers do this by inviting students to become more specific, by requesting that they elaborate or rephrase the idea, or by seeking descriptions of the thinking processes underlying the production of that idea (see chapter 5 on metacognition). The teacher may express a lack of understanding of the student's idea and seek further explanation.

The intent of clarifying is to help the teacher better understand the students' ideas, feelings, and thought processes (cognitive mapping). Clarifying is *not* a devious way to change or redirect what the student is thinking or feeling. It is *not* a way for the teacher to direct the class' attention to the "correct answer."

The clarifying process often involves an interrogative, but may also be in the form of a statement inviting further illumination. For example, the teacher might say:

"Could you explain to us what you mean by 'charisma'?"

"What you are saying is that you'd rather work by yourself than in a group. Is that correct?"

"Go over that one more time, Shelley. I'm not sure I understand you."

"You say you are studying the situation. Tell us just exactly what you do when you 'study' something."

"Explain to us in order the steps that you took to arrive at that answer."

By *clarifying*, teachers show students that their ideas are worthy of exploration and consideration; their full meaning, however, is not yet understood. Clarifying demonstrates that the teacher is interested in, wants to pursue, and values students' thinking.

It has been found that when a teacher responds to students' comments by encouraging them to elaborate further, there is a positive effect on achievement. Students become more purposeful in their thinking and behaving.

>> *Providing information*

If one of the objectives of teaching thinking is for students to process data by comparing, classifying, making inferences, or drawing causal relationships, then data must be available for the student to process. Providing information occurs when the teacher perceives the student needs information or when the student requests additional information, and the teacher *responds* by providing it or making it possible for the student to acquire the data, facts, or information needed or requested.

Creating an environment

The teacher, therefore, creates an environment that is responsive to the student's quest for information. Teachers can do this in a variety of ways:

- By providing data (feedback) about a student's performance:
  "No, three times six is not twenty-four. Three times eight is twenty-four."

"Yes, you have spelled 'rhythm' correctly."

- By providing personal information or data to students (self-divulgence, often in the form of "I" messages):

  "I want you to know that chewing gum in this classroom really disturbs me."

  "John, your pencil tapping is disturbing me."

  "The way you painted the tree makes me feel like I'm on the inside looking out."

- By making it possible for students to experiment with equipment and materials to make the critical discriminations needed to find accurate data or information for themselves:

  "Here's a larger test tube to use if you'd like to see how your experiment would turn out differently."

  "We can see the film again if you want to check your observations."

- By making primary and secondary sources of information accessible:

  "Maria, this almanac gives information you will need for your report on the world's highest mountain ranges."

  "Here's the dictionary. The best way to verify the spelling is to look it up."

- By responding to a student's request for information:

  Student: "What's this thing called?"

  Teacher: "This piece of equipment is called a 'bell jar.'"

- By surveying the group for its feelings or input of information.

  "On this chart we have made a list of what you observed in the film. We can keep this chart in front of us for a reference as we classify our observations."

  "Let's go around the circle and share some feelings we had when we learned the school board decided to close our school."

- By labeling a thinking process or behavior:

  "That is an hypothesis you are posing, Gina."

"Sharing your crayons like that is an example of cooperation, Mark."

"The question you are asking is an attempt to verify data."

- By making the distinction between feedback and rewards, a teacher can either control one's behavior (rewards), or give information about one's competence (feedback). If a student perceives the teacher's reward as controlling, a decrease in the student's intrinsic motivation will likely occur. If the student, however, perceives the reward as providing feedback about his or her knowledge or competence, an increase in intrinsic motivation is likely.

Feedback

Feedback or response to a student's behavior needs to occur in a few seconds if learning is to progress rapidly. Feedback need not always come from an external source but may arise from concepts, data, and principles recalled or gathered by the learners themselves. For example, the teacher may provide a model with which the student checks for accuracy or correctness, or the student may compare his/her work with the answers of other students or with rules stated in the instructions. In other words, the teacher needs to provide an opportunity for the student to perform an internal check of the ideas held with the data being gathered so that the students can decide for themselves if the idea or answer is correct. This self-checking can furnish some immediate feedback and satisfaction that in turn reinforce learning.

Availability of data

Data of all kinds needs to be available in great abundance. It should be possible for the inquirer to obtain whatever data he or she wants as easily and quickly as possible from many sources: manipulation of materials, tools and references, the teacher, and other resource people.

Summary

In a poll conducted by the University of Northern Colorado, 87% of the parents surveyed said that the ability to communicate, understand, and relate was a very important quality that their children's teachers should have. The Colorado Department of Education concluded that the top concern of high school students was a lack of acceptance and involvement. Students felt no one cared and no one listened to their needs (EDUCATION USA, 1978).

Probably the main reason all the open-type response behaviors described in this chapter create a warm climate for learning is that they require teachers to listen. The teacher's use of silence communicates to students the teacher's value of reflective, thoughtful, crafted answers rather than impulsive answers. The use of accepting behaviors demands that teachers be sensitive to and understand students' ideas. They signal students that the product of their minds has meaning for and influence upon another human being. Clarifying and probing demonstrate a desire to go deeper and to further explore the power of the student's ideas. Providing information requires that teachers listen to and sense the students' need for information so that proper data may be supplied. Finally, not only do these teacher behaviors create a warm climate, but also they provide a model for the rational behaviors teachers desire in students.

References

Andre, T. (1979). Does answering higher level questions while reading facilitate productive learning? *Review of Educational Research*, Spring, *49*, 280-318.

Bandura, A. and Walter, R. (1963). *Social Learning and Personality Development*. New York: Holt, Rinehart and Winston.

Belcher, T. (1975). Modeling original divergent responses: an initial investigation. *Journal of Educational Research*, *67*, 351-358.

Bloom, B. et al. (1956). *Taxonomy of Educational Objectives, Handbook I: Cognitive Domain*. New York: David McKay Co.

———— and Broder, L. (1950). *Problem-Solving Processes of College Students*. Chicago: University of Chicago Press.

Brophy, J. (1981). *Teacher praise: a functional analysis*. East Lansing: Michigan State University Institute for Research on Teaching, Occasional Paper No. 28, October.

Brown, A. (1978). Knowing when, where, and how to remember: a problem of meta-cognition. In Glaser (Ed.), *Advances in Instructional Psychology*. Hillsdale, NJ: Erlbaum.

Carin, A. and Sund, R. (1971). *Developing Questioning Technique: A Self-concept Approach*. Columbus: Charles E. Merril Co.

Costa, A. (1984). Mediating the metacognitive. *Educational Leadership*, November, *42*, 57-62.

———— (1985). Teaching behaviors that enable student thinking. In Costa (Ed.), *Developing Minds: A Resource Book for Teaching Thinking*. Alexandria, VA: Association for Supervision and Curriculum Development.

———— (1986). *The Enabling Behaviors*. Orangevale, CA: Search Models Unlimited.

Daily, F. (1970). *A study of female teacher's verbal behavior and peer-group structure among classes of fifth-grade children.* Unpublished doctoral dissertation, Kent, OH: Kent State University,

Deci, E. (1976). *Intrinsic Motivation.* New York: Plenum Press.

———— (1978). Application of research on the effect of rewards. In M. Lepper and D. Greene (Eds.), *The Hidden Costs of Rewards: New Perspective on the Psychology of Human Motivation.* New York: Erlbaum.

Dillon, J. (1984) Research on questioning and discussion, *Educational Leadership*, November, *42*.

EDUCATION, U. S. A. (1978). Arlington, VA: National School Public Relations Association, September, *4*.

Egan, K. (1975). How to ask questions to promote higher level thinking, *Peabody Journal of Education*, April.

Feuerstein, R. (1980). *Instrumental Enrichment.* Baltimore: University Park Press.

Flanders, N. (1970). *Analyzing Teacher Behavior.* Reading, MA: Addison-Wesley.

Gagne, R. (1967). *Conditions for Learning.* New York: Holt, Rinehart and Winston.

Gall, M. (1970). The use of questions in teaching. *Review of Educational Research*, December, *40*, 207-220.

Hunkins, F. (1972). *Questioning Strategies and Techniques.* Rockleigh, NJ: Allyn Bacon.

Irion, A. (1966). A brief history of research on the acquisition of skill. In E. A. Belodeau (Ed.), *Acquisition of Skill.* New York: Academic Press.

Kimble, G. and Hilgard, E. (1961). *Conditioning and Learning.* New York: Appleton-Century Crofts.

Klevan, A. (1958). *An investigation of a methodology for value clarification: its relationship to consistency of thinking, purposefulness, and human relations.* Unpublished dissertation, New York: New York University.

Lowery, L. and Marshall, H. (1979). *Learning about Instruction: Teacher Initiated Statements and Questions.* Berkeley: University of California.

——— (1980). *Learning More about Learning: Teacher Initiated Statements and Questions.* Berkeley: University of California.

Rosenshine, B. (1970). Enthusiastic teaching, a research review. *School Review, 78,* 279-301.

——— and Furst, N. (1971). Current and future research on teacher performance criteria. In B. O. Smith (Ed.), *Research on Teacher Education: A Symposium.* Englewood Cliffs, NJ: Prentice Hall.

Rowe, M. (1974). Wait time and rewards as instructional variables: their influence on language, logic and fate control. *Journal of Research in Science Teaching, 11,* 81-94.

Saunders, N. (1966). *Classroom Questions: What Kinds?* New York: Harper and Row.

Servey, R. (1974). *Teacher Talk: The Knack of Asking Questions.* Belmont, CA: Fearon Publishers.

Soar, R. (1972). Pupil teacher interaction. In J. Squire (Ed.), *A New Look at Progressive Education.* Alexandria, VA: Yearbook of the Association for Supervision and Curriculum Development.

Sprinthall, N. and Theis-Sprinthall, L. (1983). The teacher as an adult learner: a cognitive developmental view. In G. Griffin (Ed.), *Staff Development.* 82nd yearbook of the National Society for the Study of Education, Chicago: University of Chicago Press.

Suchman, J. R. (1964). *The Elementary School Training Program in Scientific Inquiry.* Urbana IL: University of Illinois.

Wallen, N. and Woodke, J. (1963). *Relationships Between Teacher Characteristics and Student Behavior, Part I*. Salt Lake City: Department of Educational Psychology, University of Utah.

Wease, H. (1976). Questioning: the genius of teaching and learning, *High School Journal*, March.

Whimbey, A. (1980). Students can learn to be better problem solvers. *Educational Leadership*, April, *37*, 56-65.

Winne, P. (1979). Experiments relating teachers' use of higher cognitive questions to student achievement. *Review of Educational Research*, Winter, *49*, 13-50.

CHAPTER 4

USING THOUGHT-FULL LANGUAGE IN THE CLASSROOM

Teacher A

"The bell has rung. It's time to go home. Clear off your desks, stand behind your chairs, and quietly slide your chairs under your desks."

Teacher B

"The bell has rung. It's time to go home. What will you need to do to get ready?"

In which of these examples of teacher language is more responsibility for thinking thrust upon the students?

∞   ∞   ∞

Language and thinking are inexorably linked. Numerous psychologists believe that language is the most important component of intelligence. Vygotsky (1962) believed that the ability to think linguistically is the most important distinction between human and animal cognition. Piaget was equally convinced of the importance of thought via language. For him (1970), children learn through "ego-centric" speech to organize the outside world and integrate it with the concept of self.

If language is central to the development of an individual's cognition, there are strong implications for classroom teachers involved in developing students' intellect. It implies that if we are to successfully develop programs and practices for teaching thinking, we must also develop a "language of cognition." Teachers must learn how to embed in their everyday classroom language opportunities for students to hear cognitive terminology and be presented with day-to-day challenges to think. Similarly, students must understand the language of thinking in order to facilitate their own cognitive growth.

This chapter will focus on ways language is used in the everyday dialogue of the classroom. If we surround students with *thought-full* language, we are using a powerful vehicle to make reflective thinking part of their everyday lives.

The Linguistic Nature of Instruction

One of the most significant findings in the current research on instructional practices is that teaching and learning are predominantly linguistic phenomena. Feuerstein (1980) describes the teacher's interactive role as crucial in the mediated learning experience of children's cognitive development. In their major review of studies of the linguistic interactions in classrooms, Green and Smith (1982) conclude that language is used by teachers to "frame" the presentation of content, the tasks students are to perform, and the norms of acceptable and unacceptable conduct. The words that teachers use communicate to students what to do, when to do it, and how to act in the process.

Condon (1968) identifies labeling as another fundamental characteristic of language and therefore relevant to classroom interaction. He states that when you create a name or a label for something, you also create a reality for yourself that previously did not exist. To illustrate, Condon uses the example of taking a course in astronomy. Before taking the course, a person will look at the nighttime sky and see only stars. After a few weeks of the course, the individual will begin to see super novae, white dwarfs, galaxies, etc. The creation of labels, then, is a tool we use to structure our perceptions. New labels foster new perceptions. As Condon says, "...for better or for worse, when names are learned we see what we had not seen for we know what to look for."

Because of the nature and importance of language, it is essential that teachers closely examine their classroom language to see that it encourages *thinking*. We need to search for opportunities to link language and thought, to redefine more precisely current terminology. Such opportunities offer the possiblility and even the occasion for inventing new language for specific classroom situations.

We believe the seven areas described below are starting places for the development of *thought-full* language. You are invited to seek other opportunities. Each will be described in brief.

Thinking Words

Teachers are often heard admonishing students to think: "Think hard." Students are sometimes criticized for not having the inclination to do so: "These kids just go off without thinking."

The term "think" is a vague abstraction covering a wide range of mental activities. Two possible reasons why students fail to engage in it are (1) the vocabulary is a foreign language to them, and (2) they may not know how to perform the specific skills that the term implies. If adults would speak with *thought-full* language—using specific thinking-skill labels and instructing students in ways to perform those skills—students, too, might be more inclined to use them. For example:

Instead of saying:	Speak *thought-fully*, saying:
"Let's look at these two pictures."	"Let's *compare* these two pictures."
"What do you think will happen when...?"	What do you *predict* will happen when...?"
"How can you put into groups...?"	"How can you *classify*...?"
"Let's work this problem."	"Let's *analyze* this problem."
"What do you think would have happened if...?"	"What do you *speculate* would have happened if...?"
"What did you think of this story?"	"What *conclusions* can you draw about this story?"
"How can you explain...?"	"What *hypotheses* do you have that might explain...?"

Instead of saying:	Speak *thought-fully*, saying:
"How do you know that's true?"	"What *evidence* do you have to support...?"
"How could you use this...?"	"How could you *apply* this?"

As children hear these thinking labels in everyday use and as they experience the cognitive processes that accompany these terms, they will internalize the words and use them as part of their own vocabulary. These are the beginnings of metacognition— awareness of their own thinking processes. Teachers will also want to provide specific instruction in those cognitive processes so that students will attach precise, shared meaning to the terms (Beyer, 1985). In chapter 6 of this book, a strategy will be described for teaching a thinking skill directly.

Discipline

When disciplining children, teachers often make decisions about which behaviors to discourage and which to reinforce. Teachers can speak *thought-fully* by posing questions that cause children to examine their own behavior, consider the consequences of that behavior, and choose more appropriate actions for themselves (Bailis and Hunter, 1985). For example:

Instead of saying:	Speak *thought-fully*, saying:
"Be quiet."	"The noise you make disturbs us. Can you work so we don't hear you?"
"Sarah, get away from Shawn."	"Sarah, can you find another place to do your best work?"
"Stop interrupting."	"It's Maria's turn to talk, so what do you need to do?"
Stop running.	"Why do we have the rule about walking in the halls?'

Discussions with children about appropriate behavior, class-room and school rules, and courtesy are necessary if students are to learn appropriate alternatives. Over time, students will build up a strong experiential background relative to behaviors which "work" within the culture of the classroom.

Providing Data, Not Solutions

We can rob children of the opportunity to take charge of their own behavior by providing solutions, consequences, and appropriate actions for them. If adults would merely make available input data for children's decision making, we could encourage children to act more autonomously, to become aware of the effects of their behavior on others, and to become more empathic by sensing verbal and nonverbal cues given by others. We can, however, speak *thought-fully* by giving data, divulging information about ourselves, or sending "I" messages. We might, for example, provide verbal cues for them, using phrases similar to the following:

When children (for example):	Speak *thoughtfully*, saying,
Make noise by tapping their pencils.	"I want you to know your pencil tapping disturbs me."
Interrupt.	"I like it when you take turns to speak."
Whine.	"It hurts my ears."
Are courteous.	"I liked your coming in so quietly and going to work."
Chew gum.	"Gum chewing in my class disturbs me."

Some children, of course, will be unable to recognize in these data cues for self-control. In such cases, we may have to step in and provide more specific directions for what would be more appropriate behavior.

Classroom Management

In communicating instructions, teachers can speak *thought-fully* by using questions which require students to identify what is needed to successfully complete a task. Too often teachers give all the information so students merely perform the task without having to infer meaning. Teachers might say, for example:

Instead of saying:	Speak *thought-fully*, saying:
"Remember to write your name in the upper right-hand corner of your paper."	"So I easily know whose paper it is, what must you remember to do?"
"For our field trip, remember to bring spending money, comfortable shoes, and a warm jacket."	"What must we remember to bring on our field trip?"
"When you leave the room to go to the library, get up quietly, take the hall pass, and don't slam the door."	"When you go to the library, what could you do when you leave that will least disturb others?"
"Get 52 cups, 26 scissors, and 78 sheets of paper. Get some butcher paper to cover the desks."	"Everyone will need two paper cups, a pair of scissors, and three sheets of paper. The desk tops will need to be protected. Can you figure out what to do?"

Probing for Specificity

Oral language is filled with omissions, generalizations, and vagueness. In other words, it is conceptual rather than operational, value laden, and sometimes deceptive. We speak *thought-fully* when we cause others to define terms, be specific about their actions, make precise comparisons, and use accurate descriptors (Laborde, 1984). For this, it is important to be alert to certain categories of vague or unspecified terms:

- universals, including "always," "never," "none," "everybody," or "all.";

- vague terms describing actions, e.g. "know about," "understand," "appreciate";
- comparators, for example, "better," "newer," "cheaper," "*more* nutritious";
- unreferenced pronouns, e.g., "they," "them," "we";
- unspecified groups, such as "the teachers," "corporations," "parents," "things";
- assumed rules or traditions, using, for example, "ought," "should," or "must."

When such words or phrases are heard in the speech or writings of others, we speak *thought-fully* by having them specify, define, or reference their terms:

When we hear:	Speak *thought-fully*, saying:
"He *never* listens to me."	"Never? Never, ever?
"*Everybody* has one."	"Everybody? Who exactly?"
"*Things* go better with..."	"Which things specifically?"
"Things *go* better with..."	"Go? Go—how, specifically?"
"Things go *better* with..."	"Better than what?"
"You *shouldn't* do that..."	"What would happen if you did?"
"The *parents*..."	"Which parents?"
"I want them to *understand*..."	"What exactly will they be doing if they understand?"
"This cereal is *more* nutritious..."	"More nutritious than what?"
"*They* won't let me..."	"Who are 'they'?"
"*Administrators*..."	"Which administrators?"

"Critical thinkers" are able to use specific terminology, refrain from overgeneralizing, and support assumptions with valid data (Ennis, 1985). Speaking *thought-fully* by having children use precise language develops those characteristics.

Metacognition

While we will explain this term in depth in the next chapter, it bears examining briefly here. Thinking about thinking begets more thinking (Costa, 1984). Having children describe the mental processes which they are using, the data which they are lacking, and the plans which they are formulating causes them to think about their own thinking—to metacogitate. Teachers can encourage students to metacogitate by encouraging them to express their inner thoughts externally. Whimbey (1985) refers to this as "Talk Aloud Problem Solving."

When children say:	Speak *thought-fully*, saying:
"The answer is 43 pounds, 7 ounces."	"Describe the steps you took to arrive at that answer."
"I don't know how to solve this problem."	"What can you do to get started?"
"I'm ready to begin."	"Describe your plan of action."
"We're memorizing our poems."	"What do you do when you memorize?"
"I like the large one best."	"What criteria are you using to make your choice?"
"I'm finished."	"How do you know you're correct?"

As teachers probe students to describe what's going on "inside their heads" when they are thinking, students become more aware of their thinking processes; and as they listen to other students describe their metacognitive processes, they develop flexibility of thought and an appreciation for the variety of ways to solve the same problem.

Analyzing the Logic of Language

Finally, *thought-full* language can be fostered by having students analyze the logic implied by certain linguistic expressions. Specifically, certain words and phrases indicate logical relationships between ideas. These relationships are usually signaled by linguistic cues. Five of the more commonly used relationships are:

Relationship	Description	Linguistic Cue
Addition	Two ideas go together in some way.	"He is intelligent *and* he is kind."
Comparison	Common attributes are shared.	"Shawn *and* Sarah *both* play the violin."
Contrast	Two ideas don't go together.	"He is healthy, *but* he doesn't exercise."
Sequence	One event happens before, during, or after another event.	"He went home, *then* he went to the library, checked out some books, and returned to school."
Causality	One event occurs as a result of another.	"*Since* no one was home, he went to the gym."

To encourage use of these relationship expressions, students can be asked to:

- identify ideas that are related within a sentence;
- identify the type of relationship between the ideas (addition, comparison, contrast, sequence, or causality);
- identify the linguistic cue for the performance of that cognitive relationship (and, or, but, after, while, etc.);
- discuss the meaning implied by these relationships.

It is believed that teaching students to be alert to the thinking processes expressed in written and spoken language can help them become aware of their own language and thought; decode the syntactic, semantic, and rhetorical signals found in all languages; and integrate the complex interaction of language, thought, and action (Marzano and Hutchins, 1985).

Summary

Language is a tool. As such, we can use it to enhance cognitive development. Speaking *thought-fully* simply means that we consciously use our language to evoke thinking in others by:

- using specific thinking terms rather than vague, abstract terms;

- posing questions that cause students to examine their own behavior, search for the consequences of that behavior, and choose more appropriate actions for themselves;

- giving data, divulging information about ourselves, or sending "I" messages so that students must "process" the information;

- causing students to analyze a task, decide on what is needed, then act autonomously;

- causing others to define their terms, become specific about their actions, make precise comparisons, and use accurate descriptors;

- causing the covert thought processes that students are experiencing to become overt (metacognition); and

- helping children study and become alert to the cues in the language structure which evoke thought processes.

By asking questions, selecting terms, clarifying ideas and processes, providing data, and withholding value judgments, we can stimulate and enhance the thinking of others. Using *thought-full* language, we can grow intelligent behavior.

References

Bailis and Hunter, M. (1985). Do your words get them to think? *Learning*, August, *14.*

Beyer, B. (1985). Practical strategies for the direct teaching of thinking skills. In Costa (Ed.), *Developing Minds: A Resource Book for Teaching Thinking.* Alexandria, VA: Association for Supervision and Curriculum Development.

Condon, J. (1968). *Semantics and Communication.* New York: MacMillan.

Costa, A. (1984). Mediating the metacognitive. *Educational Leadership,* November, *42,* 57-62.

Ennis, R. (1985). Goals for a critical thinking curriculum. In Costa (Ed.), *Developing Minds: A Resource Book for Teaching Thinking.* Alexandria, VA: Association for Supervision and Curriculum Development.

Feuerstein, R. (1980). *Instrumental Enrichment.* Baltimore: University Park Press.

Green, J. and Smith, D. C. (1982). *Teaching and learning: a linguistic perspective.* Paper presented at the Conference on Research on Teaching: Implications for Practice. February, Warrenton, VA.

Laborde, G. (1985). *Influencing with Integrity.* Palo Alto, CA: Syntony Press.

Marzano, R. and Hutchins, C. (1985). *Thinking Skills: A Conceptual Framework.* Aurora, CO: Midcontinent Regional Educational Laboratory.

Piaget, J. (1970). Piaget's theory. In Mussen (Ed.), *Carmichael's Manual of Child Psychology (Vol. 1).* New York: John Wiley and Sons.

Whimbey, A. (1985). Test results for teaching thinking. In Costa (Ed.), *Developing Minds: A Resource Book for Teaching Thinking.* Alexandria, VA: Association for Supervision and Curriculum Development.

Vygotsky, L. (1962). *Thought and Language.* Cambridge: Massachusetts Institute of Technology Press.

CHAPTER 5
METACOGNITION: THINKING ABOUT THINKING

Try to solve this problem in your head: *How much is one-half of two plus two?* Did you hear yourself talking to yourself? Did you find yourself having to decide if you should take one-half of the first two, which would give the answer three; or if you should sum the twos first, which would give the answer two?

∞ ∞ ∞

In reading the above, if you caught yourself having an "inner" dialogue, and if you had to stop to evaluate your own decision-making/problem-solving processes, you were experiencing *metacognition*. You were thinking about your own thinking.

Occurring in the neocortex of the brain and therefore thought by many neurobiologists to be uniquely human, metacognition is our ability to know what we know and what we don't know. It is our ability to plan a strategy for producing needed information, to be conscious of our own steps and strategies during the act of problem solving, and to reflect on and evaluate the productiveness of our own thinking. While "inner language," thought to be a prerequisite, begins in most children around age five, metacognition is a key attribute of formal thought, flowering about age eleven. Interestingly, not all humans achieve the level of formal operations and not all adults metacogitate (Whimbey, 1976).

Students often follow instructions or perform tasks without wondering why they are doing what they are doing. They seldom question themselves about their own learning strategies or evaluate the efficiency of their own performance. Some children virtually have no idea what they should do when confronting a problem and are often unable to explain their decision-making strategies (Sternberg and Wagner, 1982). There is much evidence, however, to demonstrate that those who perform well on complex cognitive tasks, who are flexible and perseverant in problem solving, and who consciously apply their intellectual skills are those who possess well-developed metacognitive abilities (Bloom and Broder, 1950; Brown, 1978; Whimbey, 1980). They are those who "manage" their intellectual resources well: (1) their basic perceptual-motor skills; (2) their language, beliefs, knowledge of content, and memory processes; and (3) their purposeful and voluntary strategies intended to achieve a desired outcome (Aspen Institute, 1982).

Returning to our model of thinking, we see that metacognition is an overarching cognitive ability that "monitors" our other thinking processes.

Model of Thinking

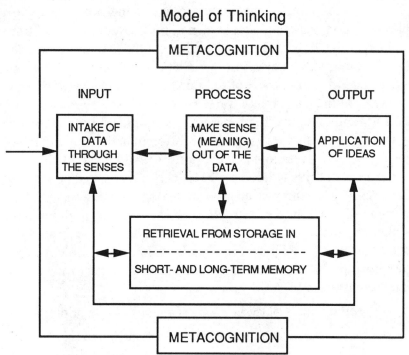

If teachers wish to develop effective thinking and intelligent behavior in students, then their instructional strategies should be purposefully designed to develop children's metacognitive abilities. Interestingly, *direct* instruction in metacognition may *not* be beneficial. When strategies of problem solving are imposed by the teacher rather than generated by the students themselves, their performance may become impaired. Conversely, when students experience the need for problem-solving strategies, induce their own, discuss and practice them to the degree that they become spontaneous and unconscious, their metacognition seems to improve (Sternberg and Wagner, 1982). The trick, therefore, is to develop students' metacognitive abilities without creating an even greater burden on their ability to attend to the task. (We discuss this point in chapter 6.)

The major components of metacognition include developing a plan of action, maintaining that plan in mind over a period of time, and then reflecting back on and evaluating the plan upon completion. Planning a strategy before embarking on a course of action assists us in keeping track of the steps in the sequence of planned behavior at the conscious-awareness level for the activity's duration. It facilitates making temporal and comparative judgments; assessing the readiness for more or different activities; and monitoring our interpretations, perceptions, decisions, and behaviors. An example of this would be what superior teachers do daily, i.e., developing a teaching strategy for a lesson, keeping that strategy in mind throughout the instruction, then reflecting back upon the strategy to evaluate it's effectiveness in producing the desired student outcomes. Rigney (1980) identified the following self-monitoring skills as necessary for successful performance on intellectual tasks:

- keeping one's place in a long sequence of operations;
- knowing that a subgoal has been obtained; and
- detecting errors and recovering from those errors either by making a "quick fix" or by retreating to the last known correct operation.

Such monitoring involves "looking ahead" *and* "looking back." "Looking ahead" includes:

- learning the structure of a sequence of operations;
- identifying areas where errors are likely;
- choosing a strategy that will reduce the possibility of error and will provide easy recovery; and
- identifying the different kinds of feedback that will be available at various points and evaluating the usefulness of that feedback.

"Looking back" includes:

- detecting errors previously made;
- keeping a history of what has been done to date and thereby what should come next; and
- assessing the reasonableness of the immediate outcome of task performance.

A simple example of this might be drawn from a reading task. It is a common experience while reading a passage to have our minds wander from the pages. We see the words, but no meaning is being produced. Suddenly we realize that we are not concentrating and that we've lost contact with the meaning of the text. We "recover" by returning to the passage to find our place, matching it with the last thought we can remember, and having found it, we read on with connectedness. This inner awareness and the strategy of recovery are components of metacognition.

Strategies for Enhancing Metacognition

Below are some teaching suggestions for enhancing metacognition. Whether teaching vocational education, physical education, algebra, or reading skills, teachers can promote metacognition by using these and similar instructional techniques.

Strategy planning. Prior to any learning activity, teachers will want to take time to develop and discuss strategies and steps for attacking problems, rules to remember, and directions to be followed. Time constraints, purposes, and ground rules under which students must operate should be developed and interiorized. Thus, students can better keep these in mind *during* and evaluate their performance *after* the experience.

During the activity, teachers may invite students to share their progress, their thought processes, and their perceptions of their own behavior. Asking students to indicate where they are in their strategy, to describe the "trail" of thinking up to that point, and to identify alternative pathways they intend to pursue next in the solution of their problem helps them become aware of their own behavior. (It also provides the teacher with a diagnostic "cognitive map" of the student's thinking, which can be used to give more individualized assistance.)

Then, *after* the learning activity is completed, teachers can invite students to evaluate how well those rules were followed, how productive the strategies were, whether the instructions were followed correctly, and what some alternative, more efficient strategies would be used in the future.

A kindergarten teacher begins and ends each day with a class meeting. During these times, children make plans for the day. They decide which learning tasks to accomplish and how to accomplish them. They allocate classroom space, assign roles, and develop criteria for appropriate conduct. Throughout the day the teacher calls attention to the plans and ground rules made that morning and invites students to compare what they are doing with what was agreed upon. Then, before dismissal, another class meeting is held to reflect on, evaluate, and plan further strategies and criteria.

Question generating. Regardless of the subject area, it is useful for students to pose study questions for themselves prior to and during their reading of textual material. This self-generation of questions facilitates comprehension. It also encourages students to pause frequently and perform a self-check for understanding to determine whether or not comprehension has actually occurred.

If, for example:

- they know the main characters or events;
- they are grasping the concept;
- it makes sense;
- they can relate it to what they already know;
- they can give other examples or instances;
- they can use the main idea to explain other ideas; or
- they can use the information in the passage to predict what may come next,

comprehension is taking place.

To increase comprehension, students must decide what strategic action should be taken to remove obstacles to this goal. After the reading, they may mentally summarize what they've read. Also, they may check to see if it makes sense and may compare what they know now with what they wanted to know before they started. This helps students become more self-aware and take conscious control of their own studying (Sanacore, 1984).

Conscious choosing. Teachers can promote metacognition by helping students explore the consequences of their choices and decisions prior to and during the act of deciding. Students will then be able to perceive causal relationships between their choices, their actions, and the results they achieved. Providing nonjudgmental feedback about the effects of their behaviors and decisions on others and on their environment helps students become aware of their own behaviors. For example, a teacher's statement, "I want you to know that the noise you're making with your pencil is disturbing me," will better contribute to metacognitive development than the command, "John, stop tapping your pencil."

Differentiated evaluations. Teachers may enhance metacognition by causing students to reflect upon and categorize their actions according to two or more sets of evaluative criteria. An example would be inviting students to distinguish what was done that day that was helpful and hindering, what they liked and didn't like, or what were the pluses and minuses of the activity. Thus, students must keep the criteria in mind, apply them to multiple classification systems, and justify their reasons accordingly.

Taking credit. Teachers may cause students to identify what they have done well and invite them to seek feedback from their peers. The teacher might ask, "What have you done that you're proud of?" and "How would you like to be recognized for doing that?" (name on the board, hug, pat on the back, handshake, applause from the group, etc.). Thus, students will become more conscious of their own behavior and will apply a set of internal criteria for that behavior which they consider "good."

Outlawing "I can't." Teachers should inform students that their excuses of "I can't...," "I don't know how to...," or "I'm too slow to..." are unacceptable behaviors in the classroom. Rather, having students identify what information is required, what materials are needed, or what skills are lacking in their ability to perform the desired behavior is an alternative and acceptable response. This helps students identify the boundaries between what they know and what they need to know. It develops a persistent attitude and enhances the student's ability to create strategies that will produce needed data.

Paraphrasing or reflecting back students' ideas. Paraphrasing, building upon, extending, and using students' ideas can make them conscious of their own thinking (see chapter 3). The teacher might say, "What you're telling me is..." or "What I hear in your plan are the following steps..." or "Let's work with Peter's strategy for a moment."

Inviting students to restate, translate, compare, and paraphrase each other's ideas causes them to become not only better listeners to other's thinking, but better listeners to their own thinking as well.

Labeling students' cognitive behaviors. When the teacher places labels on students' cognitive processes, it can make them conscious of their own actions: "What I see you doing is making out a *plan of action* for..."; "What you are doing is called an *ex-*

periment"; "You're being very helpful to Mark by sharing your paints. That's an example of *cooperation*."

Clarifying students' terminology. Students often use "hollow," vague, or nonspecific terminology. For example, in making value judgments students might be heard saying, "It's not fair..."; "He's too strict..."; "It's no good...." Teachers need to be ready to clarify these value statements: "What's *too* strict?" "What would be fairer?"

We sometimes hear students using nominalizations, e.g., "They're mean to me..."; ("Who are 'they'?") "We had to do that..."; ("Who is 'we'?") "Everybody has one..."; ("Who is 'everybody'?") Thus, clarifying causes students to operationally define their terminology and to examine the premise on which their thinking is based. It is desirable that, as a result of such clarifying, students' terminology would become more specific and qualifying.

For older children, approximately above age eleven, it appears helpful to invite them to clarify their problem-solving processes. Causing them to describe their thinking while they are in that process seems to beget more thinking. Some examples might be: inviting a student to talk aloud as he or she solves a problem; discussing what is going on in their head when, for example, they confront an unfamiliar word; or identifying the steps they use to decide whether to buy some article at the store. Confirming students' "right answers" stops metacognition; asking them, "How do you know that answer is correct?" or "What did you do to check your answers?" causes students to continue metacogitating.

After a problem is solved, the teacher can invite a clarification of the processes used: "Sarah, you figured out that the answer was 44; Shawn says the answer is 33. Let's hear how you came up with 44; retrace your steps for us." Thus, clarifying helps students re-examine their own problem-solving processes, identify their own errors, and self-correct. The teacher might ask a question, such as "How much is three plus four?" The student might reply, "twelve." Rather than merely correcting the student, the teacher might choose to clarify: "Gina, how did you arrive at that answer?"

"Well, I multiplied four and three and got.... Oh, I see, I multiplied instead of adding."

Role playing and simulations. When students assume the roles of other persons, they have to hold in mind the attributes and characteristics of that person. Dramatization serves as a hypothesis or prediction of how that person would react in a certain situation. This also contributes to the reduction of ego-centered perceptions.

Journal keeping. Writing and illustrating a personal log or a diary throughout an experience causes the student to synthesize thoughts and actions and to translate them into symbolic form. The record also provides an opportunity to revisit initial perceptions—to compare the changes in those perceptions with the addition of more data; to chart the processes of strategic thinking and decision making; to identify the blind alleys and pathways taken; and to recall the successes and the "tragedies" of experimentation. (A variation on writing journals would be making video and/or audio tape recordings of actions and performances.)

Discussing and evaluating thinking abilities admired in others. Students might reflect upon people who are considered great thinkers, e.g., Mozart, Einstein, DaVinci, or Poe. What mental prowess did they possess that yielded products of such insightfulness, fascination, and utility for others? We also want students to become aware of efficient, creative, productive thinking in people all around them: salespeople, mechanics, inventors, politicians, musicians, and yes, even parents and teachers. Such discussions may help them become aware of their own thinking, as well as the thinking of others.

Modeling. Of all the instructional techniques suggested, the one with the probability of greatest influence on students is that of teacher modeling. Since students learn best by imitating the significant adults around them, the teacher who publicly demonstrates metacognition will probably produce students who metacogitate. Some indicators of a teacher's public metacognitive behavior might include:

- sharing their planning—describing their goals and objectives and giving reasons for their actions;
- making human errors, but then being seen to recover from those errors by getting "back on track";
- admitting they do not know an answer, but designing ways to produce one;
- seeking feedback and evaluation of their actions and words from others;
- having a clearly-stated value system and making decisions consistent with that value system;
- being able to self-disclose—using adjectives that describe their own strengths and weaknesses;
- demonstrating understanding and empathy through listening to and accurately describing the ideas and feelings of others.

References

Aspen Systems. (1982). *Topics in Learning and Learning Disabilities*. April, 2, Gaithersburg, MD: Aspen Systems Corp., (entire issue).

Bloom, B. and Broder, L. (1950). *Problem-Solving Processes of College Students*. Chicago: University of Chicago Press.

Brown, A. (1978). Knowing when, where, and how to remember: a problem of metacognition. In Glaser (Ed.), *Advances in Instructional Psychology*. Hillsdale, NJ: Erlbaum.

Rigney, J. (1980). Cognitive learning strategies and qualities in information processing. In Snow, Federico, and Montague (Eds.), *Aptitudes, Learning, and Instruction, Vol. 1*. Hillsdale, NJ: Erlbaum.

Sanacore, J. (1984). Metacognition and the improvement of reading: Some important links. *Journal of Reading*, May, 706-712.

Sternberg, R. and Wagner, R. (1982). *Understanding intelligence: What's in it for education*. Paper submitted to the National Commission on Excellence in Education.

Whimbey, A. (1980). Students can learn to be better problem solvers. *Educational Leadership*, April, *37*.

———— and Whimbey, L. (1976). *Intelligence Can Be Taught*. New York: Bantam Books.

CHAPTER 6

TEACHING A THINKING SKILL OR STRATEGY DIRECTLY

Mrs. Englander, the kindergarten teacher, stood erect before the children. Her arms were folded tightly across her chest; her lips were tightened and curled down at the ends. Below a wrinkled forehead and depressed eyebrows, two squinting dark eyes stared piercingly at the children.

"What's wrong?" one child inquired.

"Are you mad at us?"

"Don't you feel well?"

"Is there something wrong?"

"Are you angry?"

"Did you get up on the wrong side of the bed?" they asked.

"Today we're going to learn what an *inference* is," began Mrs. Englander.

Mrs. McDaniels, the Home Arts teacher, placed the box of breakfast cereal on the counter for all the class to see.

"Today," she began, "we're going to learn about inference by analogy."

"The Breakfast of Peak Performers" emblazoned the brightly-colored box. A picture of Harry Schwartzberger, the football hero, appeared on the back. Mrs. McDaniels structured the group activity:

"In your table groups, I'd like you to discuss the following questions."

She raised the screen to reveal some thought-provoking questions written on the board.

(1) "Do you think Harry eats this cereal? Why or why not? Is there any place on the box that says he does?"

(2) "If we compare what we've learned previously about nutrition with the list of ingredients on the box, how would a breakfast of this cereal contribute to peak performance?"

(3) "Can you give reasons why Harry's picture appears on the back of the box?"

(4) "List other examples in which heroes or other beautiful people appear in advertisements."

∞   ∞   ∞

Does the curriculum of your school include learning how to divide? Does it include learning how to *infer*? Does it include learning how to multiply? Does it include learning how to *compare*? To *generalize*? To *prioritize*?

Why Teach Thinking Directly

We may find a science textbook which asks students to make a *conclusion* based upon data observed during an experiment. We assume students know how to draw conclusions, yet we seldom teach students that skill. We may hear ourselves or other teachers ask questions similar to those below that presuppose students' knowing how to perform certain thinking skills:

"Who can summarize some of the things we've learned about the nomads of the desert?"

"Let's analyze this problem."

"How does Jamie's report compare with Shannon's?"

While we may assume that students know how to perform the basic thinking skills involved in learning the subject matter and the instructional interactions being used in the classroom, we often find this is not true. As a result, students are often dismayed, confused, and handicapped when asked, for example, to summarize, analyze, or compare. We propose, however, that students have a right to be able to employ thinking skills if they are a prerequisite to success.

If learning to think is to become a reality in education, then we believe classroom time should be devoted to teaching thinking skills directly. Teaching the processes of thinking should become the content of instruction. Like any skill, it needs to be taught and coached. It should be practiced across a variety of situations and applied to conditions beyond the context in which it was learned.

When thinking skills are taught directly, academic achievement seems to increase (DeBono, 1984; Whimbey, 1985; Feuerstein, 1980). Advocates (such as Barry Beyer, 1985) of the direct teaching of thinking skills report that performance on tests increases when time is taken to teach thinking. Furthermore, it signals the students what is important. When time is devoted to lessons on thinking, students receive the message that thinking is an important component of education.

Each of these leaders in teaching thinking, however, interprets the direct instruction of a thinking skill differently. Some advocates believe that specific skills (e.g., comparing, classifying, or the different forms of inferring based on the use of evidence) need to be defined, analyzed, and taught step-by-step. Others believe that this approach is too mechanical and analytical; that seldom do we ever just "compare"; and that thinking skills should be taught in a more nondirected, holistic way. Still others believe that certain intellectual functions are necessary for efficient, autonomous thinking and that these skills need to be remediated if they are diagnosed as deficient or instilled if they are absent.

Questions have also been raised about a conflict between this way of teaching thinking skills directly—sometimes called a "deductive" approach—and the use of important metacognitive techniques in which students themselves are asked to reflect on what they do when they use such thinking skills (Sternberg and Wagner, 1982).

The approach advocated in this book represents a middle position. We suggest that when a particular thinking process is required for successful performance of an academic task, the terminology be explained and the mental processes be actively experienced and analyzed by the students. This will increase chances they will succeed in accomplishing the academic task and will facilitate transfer, too.

Process as Content

When teaching a thinking skill directly, the content becomes the vehicle for thinking. Consonant with some of the suggestions made in the first volume of this series, traditional instructional content should be used as much as possible. For example, students can learn the process of *classifying* using this week's spelling list. We can teach *comparison* during a handwriting lesson in which students learn how to form a "d" and a "b." Students can be taught to distinguish *fact* and *opinion* during current events in the social studies class. We want students to master the content, but we can also seize opportunities in the academic learning process to teach a thinking skill directly. Restructuring the use of traditional curriculum—while not the only way to bring teaching for thinking into the classroom—provides the classroom teacher with a rich array of content and raw material with which to teach thinking.

When to Teach a Thinking Skill Directly

Thinking skills are best taught directly when:

(1) students are developmentally ready for that form of thinking. It does little good, for example, to teach students in kindergarten or first grade to classify simultaneously, using multiple classification systems and several sources of data. Simple classification may be performed by kindergarten and first-grade children, but materials appropriate for their developmental level must be employed.

(2) the thinking skill is relevant to and will be used successfully and repeatedly in immediate and future lessons. Teaching thinking skills once and in isolation from a meaningful context is of little educational value. While it may be a joyous experience, there will be greater transfer if the students see how it will help

them and if there will be several occasions in the near future to revisit, practice, and apply that skill. Thinking skills should be taught in ways that are accompanied by deliberate teaching for transfer through repeated practice using the same skills.

Model of Thinking

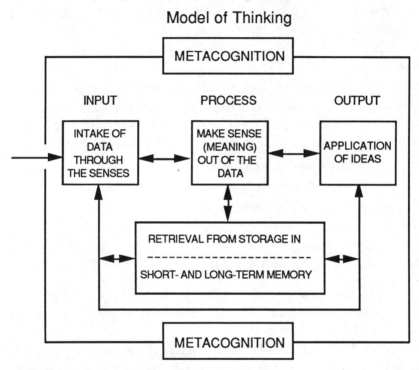

Below are descriptions of

- a lesson-planning strategy designed for teaching a thinking skill directly,
- several suggested lessons intended to illustrate that lesson design, and
- ways you may search for other opportunities to teach a thinking skill directly.

A Lesson-Planning Strategy
For Teaching a Thinking Skill Directly

This lesson design is based upon the model of thinking presented earlier in this book and is included below for review and easy reference.

As we indicated earlier, this model is designed as our instructional model. It filters out of the complex web of activities that go on when we think of those key ingredients that should be the focus of thinking-skill instruction. Using it as a guide, what follows is a generic lesson plan for teaching a thinking skill directly. It is based upon four major steps.

>>   *Input.* During this stage the teacher calls attention to the specific thinking skill or strategy that will be the focus of the lesson. The teacher should explain that learning how to perform the thinking skill is the objective of the lesson and that the lesson will also include knowing why it is an important skill to learn, when it is to be used, and so on. The thinking skill to be learned may be

- explicated by the teacher or the students,
- recalled if students have previous experience with it,
- modeled by the teacher using familiar content,
- observed as the teacher, student, or skilled person performs it, and
- discussed by the observers.

Furthermore, vocabulary related to this skill should be built —antonyms, synonyms, similar words or processes, and related words should be introduced.

>>   *Process.* The class may be organized into small groups to actually *experience* the skill. A task, using familiar content, should be provided in which the performance of the skill is required. Students should be asked to think about their own thinking while they are performing the task.

During this phase the students should become conscious of and discuss the *metacognitive* elements of the thinking skill, e.g., what goes on in their heads when this thinking skill is being performed? What are the steps in the process?

A *thinking observer* could be appointed to record what the group members did while they were completing the task. When the group has completed the task, ask them to reflect on and *analyze* their thinking. With the help of the observer, discuss what went on inside their heads as they were completing the task.

Ask them to *sequence* their metacognitive steps: what was the first thing they did? What came next? Then what?....

>> *Output*. During this phase, students should perform the skill again but in a new setting. The content should be changed but the skill should be used again beyond the context in which it was learned. This time it could be performed individually.

The teacher could ask the students to be metacognitively aware of their own thought processes while they are completing the task. Their earlier descriptions of what they did during the *process* phase should be compared and refined.

To complete this phase, the skill should be bridged or *transferred* to other uses in school subjects, life situations, or careers. Students may be asked how they would use this skill in other subject areas, in other classes, at home or play, or with friends. They could describe professions or careers in which workers use this skill daily. In addition, drawing upon one of the suggestions in volume one in this series, other teachers can reinforce this process by also helping students to apply the skill in their own classroom settings in coordination with the direct teaching (Swartz and Perkins, 1989).

>> *Retrieval*. Soon after the skill is taught and periodically throughout the year, it needs to be reviewed when it is required in a learning task. As opportunities arise in future lessons, a brief review may be required.

The intent of teaching thinking skills directly is to cause students to use them automatically—spontaneously, without the teacher's intervention. Teachers will want to be on the lookout for instances in which students voluntarily perform the skills they were taught previously so that those skills can be reinforced.

The following pages contain an example of a lesson plan, the purpose of which is to teach a particular thinking skill, classification/categorization. While space does not allow a separate lesson plan for each thinking skill, the intent is to provide a model on which similar lesson plans might be built. Following the lesson-plan model are some suggestions and resources we offer for adding to your repertoire of thinking-skill lesson plans.

SAMPLE LESSON FOR TEACHING
A THINKING SKILL DIRECTLY

THINKING SKILL: Classification/Categorization

INPUT:

Focus: *Tell the students that the purpose of the lesson is to learn what it means to categorize and to classify and why it is necessary to learn such skills.*

Vocabulary: classify, attribute, group, sort, categorize, characteristic, compare, contrast

Ask them to discuss, define, and distinguish the meanings of the words **classify, categorize, sort,** *and* **group** *(dictionaries will be helpful).*

> To **classify** means to arrange objects into groups based upon similarities *and* to label those groups, using a name that implicitly carries the significant attributes of the group members.
>
> *Citrus*, for example, is a label given to a class of fruit. No other fruits have the same attributes of citrus other than those members of that class.
>
> To **categorize** means that the label is given and it is your responsibility to list members of that group. When I say "root vegetables," for example, what can you list under that label (carrots, beets, radishes, etc.)?
>
> To **sort** means to take from a collection of random objects and to put those items together that have like characteristics, for example, sorting laundry according to permanent press, colored, whites, etc.
>
> To **group** means to assemble those items based upon some common characteristics or attributes.

Exemplify classifying and categorizing by giving a list of familiar fruits, for example:

grapefruit	lemon	peach
apricot	plum	pear
nectarine	apple	lime
cherry	orange	tangerine

*Ask them to put all those that are alike together and to give that group a **label**:*

citrus	**stone fruit**	**core (pom)**
grapefruit	apricot	pear
orange	plum	apple
lemon	peach	
lime	cherry	
tangerine	nectarine	

*Ask them then to **categorize**. Give them the labels, **root vegetables** and **leafy vegetables**. Invite them to generate examples of items in each category.*

Process: Present a list of words. It could be the week's spelling list or a list of vocabulary words from the science or social studies textbook. Ask students to work in small groups to classify the words and to think about what goes on in their heads when they classify.

segment	finger	corner	angle
shoulder	line	square	surface
machine	magnet	reel	
circle	strut	wheel	
plane	stomach	mouth	

There is not one correct way to classify this list. What is important is that students experience the process of classification and that they justify their choice of groups and labels. The list below represents only one of many possible classifications.

mechanical words	human body	geometric terms
machine	shoulder	segment
plane	finger	circle
reel	mouth	plane
strut	stomach	line
magnet		square
wheel		angle
		surface
		corner

Ask the students and the thinking-process observer to share what they did when they classified (metacognition). Record their contributions randomly, as they are given, on an overhead, a chart, or the board. They may look something like this:

When we classify, we

- scan the list;
- look for similarities between the words;
- try a label to see if there are other words it might fit;
- define the words;
- fit other words—having found a label—into that group;
- decide what to do with words that fit more than one category (plane);
- decide what to do with words that are "left over";
- subclassify words within categories;
- expand the label to fit other words in the list;
- check to see that all words are accounted for;
- call on previous knowledge of what words mean;
- decide a purpose for classifying words.

Next, ask the students to reflect on the sequence of steps: what did they do first, second, etc. Refine the list accordingly.

OUTPUT:

Now, invite the students to apply what they have learned about classifying to a new situation (teach for transfer).

Ask your students for some help in straightening up your desk drawers (or cupboards or storage closets).

Divide the class into three or four groups or teams. Assign each team a drawer, a cupboard, or a closet. Ask them to take all the objects out and classify them. Again appoint a thinking-process observer to collect data about the group's metacognitive steps in completing the task.

When the tasks are complete, ask the groups to discuss their classifications and what they did in the process of classifying. Return to the list of metacognitive operations generated in the processing phase.

Refine the list as needed. Ask students to bridge to other subject areas: When else do they need to classify? How would it help them if they kept the steps of classification in mind as they performed a learning task?

Ask students to bridge to other times outside of school when they need to classify (allocating allowance, going to the supermarket, using the library, etc.).

Invite students to think about professions and careers in which classification is essential (postal workers, librarians, salespeople, zoo keepers, etc.).

Ask students to identify examples of classification systems they use (zip codes, Dewey Decimal System, area codes, etc.).

REVIEW:

As other learning experiences requiring classification and categorization abilities are encountered in the curriculum, have students recall what it means to classify. Review what they must keep in mind during the learning. Encourage students to use the terminology correctly, distinguishing precise meanings between such words as: classification, categorization, sorting, grouping.

In a science lesson, for example, students might be asked to categorize objects into solids, liquids and gasses. Before they begin the task, review with them the definitions and the steps in the process of categorization.

Ways Teachers Can Add to Their Teaching Of Thinking Skills Directly

After trying the above lesson-design format, you may wish to add to your list and develop lesson plans around other discrete skills and strategies. It is fairly easy to do if you will be conscious of your own thinking processes.

You already use many of the important thinking skills in your own lives, especially in your professional work. For example, as a teacher you *plan* lessons, *classify/group* students according to certain attributes, *experiment* with certain classroom arrangements, and *collect data* about their effects on student performance. After a lesson you *analyze* why the lesson worked or why it didn't. You *evaluate* students according to certain internal or external criteria, and you *prioritize* the most important learnings according to goals and available time.

Keep track of what you do when you think critically or creatively. Be metacognitively aware of the metacognitive components in the process. The next time you have a problem to solve, a special lesson to plan, or a particularly challenging situation which "taxes" your mind, keep track of the thinking processes you employ. How do you solve the problem step by step? Be especially aware of the thinking skills you are using and how you use them.

Examine your texts, other instructional materials, and teachers' guides. Make a list of all the "thinking" words, such as: *conclusions, main idea, analyze, explain*, and *compare*. Look up the definitions for these words in a dictionary. You can plan a lesson around each.

Be conscious of your own language or, better yet, turn on a tape recorder in your classroom. Listen to your own language for your use of thinking words, such as *summarize, prioritize, hypothesize, relate, analyze, problem solve*, and *make decisions*. Check to see if your students can define them. Do they know what to do when *prediction*, for example, is required in a given task? Talk it over and then give them a problem. Discuss the process of *predicting*.

Talk over your lesson plans with another teacher. Ask your colleague to force you to be as specific as possible about what your students will be doing and thinking in the lesson. For example, you might say, "I want my students to derive the formula for π (pi)." Your colleague would clarify, "What do you mean, 'derive a formula'? What goes on in your head when you *derive* something?"

After you consciously track your thinking in this way, you can then translate this into learning opportunities for students. For example, look at the numerical progression below. Be conscious of your metacognitive process when you predict what the next number/letter combination will be:

$$20\,C \quad 18\,E \quad 16\,G \quad 14\,I$$

Or, you could consider the following. When you predict the consequences of some action you are considering, what do you do when you try to do this well?

Doing this with each skill and important thinking activity which you use yourself can provide you with an understanding of thinking that can be the basis for your own lesson designs in teaching for thinking.

References

Bellanca J. and Fogarty, R. (1986). *Mental Menus: 243 Explicit Thinking Skills.* Chicago: Illinois Renewal Institute.

Beyer, B. (1985). Practical strategies for the direct teaching of thinking skills. In Costa (Ed.), *Developing Minds: A Resource Book for Teaching Thinking.* Alexandria, VA: Association for Supervision and Curriculum Development.

———— (1987). *Practical Strategies for the Teaching of Thinking.* Boston: Allyn and Bacon, Inc.

DeBono, E. (1984). Critical thinking is not enough. *Educational Leadership*, September, *42*, 16-18.

Feuerstein, R. (1980). *Instrumental Enrichment.* Baltimore: University Park Press.

Sternberg, R. and Wagner, R. (1982). *Understanding intelligence: what's in it for education?* Paper submitted to the National Commission on Excellence in Education.

Swartz, R. and Perkins, D. (1989). *Teaching Thinking: Issues and Approaches.* Pacific Grove, CA: Midwest Publications.

Whimbey, A. (1985). Test results from teaching thinking. In Costa (Ed.), *Developing Minds: A Resource Book for Teaching Thinking*, Alexandria, VA: Association for Supervision and Curriculum Development.

CHAPTER 7

HOW WE KNOW STUDENTS ARE GETTING BETTER AT THINKING

*How much we evaluate how well we teach what's
not worth learning.*

Elliot Eisner

∞   ∞   ∞

When we consider ways to collect evidence of student achievement, we probably think of testing—using some form of paper-and-pencil instrument to determine how many questions a student answers correctly. Elsewhere in this series, major attention is paid to assessing children's growth in cognitive ablilites.

As we adopt the educational goal of developing students' thinking abilities, we also need to adopt a new vision of assessment. While some types of thinking are observable, measurable, and quantifiable, we must now change that behavioristic view to focus on covert, mental, nonquantifiable processes. Educators need a "paradigm shift" as we think about ways to assess learners' growth in thinking skills.

In teaching for thinking, we are less interested in how many answers students know and more interested in observing how they behave when they *don't* know. Intelligent behavior is performed in response to questions and problems the answers to which are *not* immediately known. We are interested in observing how students produce knowledge rather than how they merely reproduce knowledge.

By definition, a problem is any stimulus, question, task, or phenomenon, the explanation for which is not immediately known. Thus, we are interested in assessing student performance under those challenging conditions which demand strategic reasoning, insightfulness, perseverance, creativity, and craftsmanship to resolve the problem.

We suggest that the best way to gather evidence of student growth is for teachers to engage in "kid watching." As students interact with real-life, day-to-day classroom problems, you will want to collect anecdotes and examples of written and visual expression that indicate students' increased growth in intelligent behavior. Records of increasing voluntary and spontaneous performance of intelligent behavior could provide more useable information about students' growth than the usual norm-referenced, multiple-choice standardized tests.

What might teachers search for as indicators that their instructional efforts are paying off? Below are fourteen suggested characteristics of intellectual growth which teachers can observe and record. The list is a synthesis of ideas from several authors who have studied and analyzed efficient, productive, and creative thinkers (Glatthorn and Baron, 1985; Perkins, 1985; Sternberg, 1986; Feuerstein, 1980). This list is not complete. You will want to think and study more about intelligent behavior and add indicators of growth you discover in students' thinking abilities.

Persistence: Persevering When the Solution To a Problem Is *Not* Immediately Apparent

Students often give up in despair when the answer to a problem is not immediately known. They often crumple their papers and throw them away saying, "I can't do this," or "It's too hard"; or they write down any answer to finish the task as quickly as possible. They lack the ability to analyze a problem in order to develop a system, structure, or strategy of problem attack.

Students demonstrate growth in thinking abilities by increasing their use of alternative strategies for problem-solving. They collect evidence to indicate if their problem-solving strategy is working, and if one strategy doesn't work, they know how to back up and try another. Often, they realize that their theory or idea must be rejected and another employed. Over time, they develop systematic methods of analyzing a problem, knowing ways to begin and what steps must be performed and what data needs to be generated or collected. This is what is meant by perseverance.

Decreasing Impulsivity

Often students blurt out the first answer that comes to mind. Sometimes they shout out an answer, start to work without fully understanding the directions, lack an organized plan or strategy for approaching a problem, and/or make immediate value judgements about an idea—criticizing or praising it—before fully understanding it. They may take the first suggestion given or operate on the first idea that comes to mind rather than considering alternatives and consequences of several possible decisions.

As students become less impulsive, we can observe them

- making fewer erasures on their papers;
- gathering much information before they begin a task;
- taking time to reflect on an answer before giving it;
- making sure they understand directions before beginning a task;
- listening to alternative points of view;
- planning a strategy for solving a problem.

Listening to Others—
With Understanding and Empathy

Some psychologists believe that the ability to listen to another person, to empathize with and to understand their point of view, is one of the highest forms of intelligent behavior. Being able to paraphrase another person's ideas; detecting indicators (cues) of the feelings or emotional states in the oral and body language of another person (empathy); accurately expressing another person's concepts, emotions and problems—all are indications of listening behaviors. Piaget called it "overcoming egocentrism."

Some children ridicule, laugh at, or put down other students' ideas. They are unable to build upon, consider the merits of, or operate on another person's ideas. We will know students' listening skills are improving when they can attend to another person and demonstrate an understanding of and empathy with that person's ideas or feelings by paraphrasing them accurately, and by building upon, clarifying, or exemplifying them.

We should be looking for students to say, "Peter's idea is..., but Sarah's idea is..."; or "Let's try Shelley's idea and see if it works"; or "Let me show you how Gina solved the problem, and then I'll show you how I solved it." Then we'll know students are listening to and internalizing others' ideas and feelings.

Flexibility in Thinking

Some students have difficulty in considering alternative points of view or dealing with several sources of information simultaneously. *Their* way to solve a problem seems to be the *only* way. *Their* answer is the only correct answer. Instead of being challenged by the process of *finding* the answer, they are more interested in knowing whether their answer is correct. Unable to sustain a process of problem solving over time, they avoid ambiguous situations. A need for certainty outweighs an inclination to doubt. Their minds are made up, and they resist being influenced by data or reasoning which contradicts their beliefs.

As students become more flexible in their thinking, they can be heard considering, expressing, or paraphrasing another person's point of view or rationale. They can give several ways to solve the same problem and can evaluate the merits and consequences of two or more alternate courses of action. When making decisions, they will often use such words or phrases as "however," "on the other hand," or "If you look at it another way...." While they progressively develop a set of moral principles to govern their own behavior, they can also change their minds in light of convincing data, arguments, or rationale. Working in groups, they often resolve conflicts through compromise, express a willingness to experiment with another person's idea, and strive for consensus.

Metacognition: Awareness of Our Own Thinking

Some people are unaware of their own thinking processes. They start to solve a problem without a plan. If they do have a plan, they are unable to determine if it is working or if it should be discarded and another plan employed. Seldom do they evaluate their strategy to determine its efficacy or efficiency.

When asked, "How are you solving that problem?" they may reply, "I don't know, I'm just doing it." They are unable to describe the steps and sequences they are using before, during, and after the act of problem solving. They cannot transform into words the visual images held in their minds. It is hard for them to plan for, reflect on, and evaluate the quality of their own thinking skills and strategies.

We can determine if students are becoming more aware of their own thinking as they are able to describe what goes on in their heads when they think. When asked, they can describe what they know and what they need to know. They can describe what data are lacking and their plans for producing those data. Before they begin to solve a problem, they can describe their plan of action, list the steps and tell where they are in the sequence of a problem-solving strategy, and trace the pathways and blind alleys they took on the road to a problem solution.

As they describe their thinking skills and strategies, they can apply cognitive vocabulary correctly. We will hear them using such terms and phrases as: "I have a hypothesis..."; "My theory is..."; "When I compare these points of view..."; "By way of summary..."; "What I need to know is..."; "The assumptions on which I am working are...."

Checking for Accuracy and Precision

Students are often careless when turning in their completed work. When asked if they have checked over their papers, they may say, "No, I'm done." They seem to feel little inclination to reflect upon the accuracy of their work, contemplate their precision, or take pride in their accomplishments. The desire to finish the task surpasses their interest in craftsmanship.

We can observe students growing in their desire for accuracy as they take time to check over their tests and papers and grow more conscientious about precision, clarity, and perfection. In order to confirm their finished product, they go back over the rules by which they were to abide, the models and visions they were to follow, and the criteria they were to employ.

Questioning and Problem Posing

One of the characteristics that distinguishes humans from other life forms is our inclination and ability to *find* problems to solve. Yet often students depend on others to solve problems, find answers, and ask questions for them. They sometimes are reluctant to ask questions for fear of displaying ignorance.

Over time, there should be an observable shift from teacher- to student-originated questions and problems. Furthermore, the types of questions students ask should change and become more specific and profound. There will be, for example, requests for data to support others' conclusions and assumptions. Such questions as, "What evidence do you have?" or "How do you know that's true?" will increasingly be heard.

More hypothetical problems will be posed. These are characterized by "If" questions: "What do you think would happen *if…?*" or "*If* that is true, then is…?"

We want students to recognize discrepancies and phenomena in their environment and to inquire into their causes. "Why do cats purr?" "How high can birds fly?" "Why does the hair on my head grow so fast, but the hair on my arms and legs grow so slowly?" "What would happen if we put the salt-water fish in a fresh-water aquarium?" "What are some alternative solutions, besides war, to international conflicts?"

Drawing on Past Knowledge and Experiences

Too often students begin each new task as though for the very first time. Teachers are often dismayed when they invite students to recall how they solved a similar problem previously and students don't remember. It would seem they had never heard of it before, even though they very recently had the same type of problem. Sometimes each experience seems encapsulated without relationship to anything that came before or that comes afterward.

Thinking students learn from experience. They are able to abstract meaning from one experience, keep it in mind, and apply it to the next experience. Students can be observed growing in this ability when heard to say, "This reminds me of..." or "This is just like the time when I...." Analogies and references to previous experiences are a part of their explanations. They call upon their store of knowledge and experience as sources of data to support, theories to explain, or processes to solve each new challenge.

Transference beyond the Learning Situation

Probably the ultimate goal of teaching is for the students to apply school-learned knowledge to real-life situations and to content areas beyond that in which it was taught. Yet we find that while students can pass mastery tests in mathematics, for example, they often have difficulty deciding whether to buy six items for $2.39 or seven for $2.86 at the supermarket.

When parents and other teachers report how they have observed students thinking at home or in other classes, we know students are transferring. For example, parents report increased interest in school, more planning in their child's use of time and finances, and more organization of their room, their books, and their belongings at home. (A parent reported that during a slumber party his daughter invited her friends to "brainstorm" which activities and games they preferred. This came after she learned brainstorming techniques in school.)

We might hear, for example, the social studies teacher describe how a student used a problem-solving strategy which was originally learned in the science class. The wood shop teacher might tell how a student volunteered a plan to measure accurately before cutting a piece of wood: "Measure twice and cut once"—an axiom learned in the math class.

Precision of Language and Thought

Some students' language is confused, vague, or imprecise. They describe attributes of objects or events with such non-specific words as "weird," "nice," or "O.K." Names for objects are, typically, "stuff," "junk," and "things." Their sentences are often punctuated with "ya' know," "er," and "uh."

We may hear vague nouns and pronouns—"*They* told me to," "*Everybody* has one," "*Teachers* don't understand me." Verbs are often nonspecific—"Let's *do* it." Comparators go unqualified —"This soda is *better*," " I like it *more*."

As students' language becomes more precise, we will hear them using more descriptive words to distinguish attributes. They will use more correct names, and when universal labels are unavailable, they will use analogies such as "crescent-shaped," or "like a bow tie." Spontaneously, they will provide criteria for their value judgments, describing why they think one product is *better* than another. Instead of using incomplete sentences, they will speak in complete sentences, voluntarily provide supportive evidence for their ideas, and elaborate, clarify, and operationally define their terminology. Their oral and written expressions will become more concise, descriptive, and coherent.

Using All the Senses

All information enters the brain through the sensory pathways: visual, tactile, kinesthetic, auditory, olfactory, and gustatory. Most language and cultural and physical learning is derived from the environment by observing or intaking through the senses.

To know a wine it must be drunk; to know a role it must be acted; to know a game it must be played; to know a dance it must be executed; to know a goal it must be envisioned. Those whose sensory pathways are open, alert, and acute absorb more information from the environment than those whose pathways are withered, immune, and oblivious to sensory stimuli.

We can observe students using all the senses as they touch, feel, and rub various objects in their environment. (Young children may put things in their mouths.) "Read me a story," they will say again and again. With the same enthusiasm, they will act out roles and "be" the thing—a fish or a flatbed or a father. "Let me see, let me see"; "I want to feel it"; "Let me try it"; "Let me hold it..." they will plead.

As they mature, we can observe that they conceive and express many ways of solving problems by use of the senses: making observations, gathering data, experimenting, manipulating, scrutinizing, identifying variables, interviewing, breaking problems down into components, visualizing, role playing, illustrating, or model building. Their expressions will use a range and variety of sensory words: "I *feel* like..."; "That *touches* me"; "I *hear* your idea"; "It leaves a bad *taste* in my mouth"; "Do you see the *picture*?"

A Sense of Humor

> "I bought my grandson some war toys; you know, rocket launchers, laser guns, 'Star-Wars' stuff. Gee, they were realistic: expensive, complicated, and they didn't work."

Smiles and laughter are exceptional human responses. They have positive effects on physiological functions, causing a drop in pulse rate, the secretion of endorphins, and increased oxygen levels in the blood. They have been found to provoke higher level thinking and to liberate creativity, including such thinking skills as anticipation, finding novel relationships, and visual imaging.

The acquisition of a sense of humor follows a developmental sequence similar to that of Piaget and Kohlberg. We may observe some students whose senses of humor have not yet been fully developed. They laugh for all the wrong reasons and often at the expense of others. They may be able to laugh at "slapstick style" visual humor, but fail to recognize a humorous situation in a story or in a verbal remark. They make up their own "jokes" which lack any humor or they make cruel fun of others' human frailty.

Human beings who behave intelligently have the ability to perceive situations from an original and often humorous vantage point. They tend to initiate humor more often, to place greater value on having a sense of humor, to appreciate and understand others' humor more, and to be more playful verbally when interacting with others. They thrive on finding incongruity and have that whimsical frame of mind characteristic of creative problem solvers (Cornett, 1986).

Wonderment, Inquisitiveness, Curiosity, And the Enjoyment of Problem Solving

Some children and adults avoid problems. We may hear them saying: "These types of thinking games turn me off"; "I was never good at these brain teasers"; or "Go ask your father, he's the brain in this family." While attending high school or college, many people never enroll in math class or another "hard" academic subjects after completing their required courses. Thinking is perceived as hard work, and people therefore recoil from "too demanding" situations.

We want to observe students growing not only in ability to use thinking skills but also in their enjoyment of problem solving. Students begin seeking problems to solve themselves and to submit to others. They will make up problems to solve on their own and request them from others. Furthermore, students will solve problems with increasing independence—without the teacher's help or intervention. Such statements as, "Don't tell me the answer; I can figure it out by myself," will indicate growing autonomy. They truly will be lifelong learners.

We will want to observe children as they commune with the world around them. Do we notice them reflecting on the changing formations of a cloud? Being charmed by the opening of a bud? Sensing the logical simplicity of mathematical order? Do they find beauty in a sunset, intrigue in the geometrics of a spider web, and exhilaration in the iridescence of a hummingbird's wings? Do they see the congruity and intricacies in the derivation of a mathematical formula? Recognize the orderliness and adroitness of a chemical change? Commune with the serenity of a distant constellation?

It is important that we observe and nurture these aesthetic instincts in students. Also, as they advance to higher grade levels, they can be seen deriving more pleasure from thinking. Their curiosity will become stronger as the problems they encounter become more complex. Their environment will elicit their inquiries as their senses capture the rhythm, patterns, shapes, colors, and harmonies of the universe. When they are able to understand the need for protecting their environment, they will display cognizant and compassionate behavior toward other life forms; respect the roles and values of other human beings; and perceive the delicate worth, uniqueness, and relationships of everything and everyone they encounter. Wonderment, a sense of awe, passion—these are the prerequisites for higher-level thinking.

Cooperative Thinking—Social Intelligence

We are social beings. We congregate in groups, find it therapeutic to be listened to, draw energy from each other, and seek reciprocity. We generously contribute time and energy when tasks are performed in groups. We would rapidly tire of those same tasks, however, if we were working alone. (One of the cruelest forms of punishment we can inflict is solitary confinement.)

Humans who behave intelligently realize that all of us are more powerful than any one of us. Probably the foremost intelligent behaviors for the postindustrial society will be a heightened ability to think in concert with others. Because we will be living in increasingly closer proximity, with the world population steadily increasing and the earth as a closed ecological system, sensitivity to others will be paramount for human survival.

Problem solving has become so complex that no one person can do it alone. No one has access to all the data needed to make critical decisions; no one person can consider as many alternatives as several people. Working in groups necessitates the ability to justify ideas and to test the feasibility of solution strategies on others. Indeed, there are not many decisions any of us make without having to consider their effects on others.

Students do not necessarily come to school knowing how to work effectively in groups. They may exhibit competitiveness, narrowness of viewpoint, egocentrism, ethnocentrism, criticism of others' values, emotions, and beliefs.

Cooperative skills need to be taught directly and practiced repeatedly. Listening, consensus seeking, giving up an idea to work on someone else's idea, empathy, compassion, leadership, knowing how to support group efforts, altruism—all are behaviors indicative of intelligent human beings.

Summary

This list of "Intelligent Behaviors" is not exhaustive. There are many other indicators of development and growth, including

- envisioning, clarifying, and defining a goal before embarking on a course of action;
- exploring the consequences of those various courses of action;
- taking risks; and
- producing creative, novel, resourceful, imaginative ideas and products.

We have presented this list to help teachers become alert to indicators of intelligent behavior. This will enable them to observe students performing them in problem situations in everyday classroom situations. Teachers might wish to elicit such a list from students or share these descriptors with them. In this way students, too, may monitor their own behavior. They may also use the list as a basis for observing and analyzing the thoughtful action of others. Teachers may wish to keep check lists, anecdotal records, and vignettes of critical incidents in which these behaviors are displayed.

Teachers may also wish to incorporate these indicators into their reports and conferences with parents. Parents, too, might be involved in collecting evidence of the performance and growth of these behaviors at home.

More importantly, teachers will want to model these attributes in their own behaviors as well.

References

Cornett, C. (1986). *Learning through Laughter; Humor in the Classroom.* Bloomington, IA: Phi Delta Kappa Educational Foundation.

Feuerstein, R. (1980). *Instrumental Enrichment.* Baltimore: University Park Press.

Glatthorn, A. and Baron, J. (1985). The good thinker. In Costa (Ed.), *Developing Minds: A Resource Book for Teaching Thinking.* Alexandria, VA: The Association for Supervision and Curriculum Development.

Perkins, D. (1985). What creative thinking is. In Costa (Ed.), *Developing Minds: A Resource Book for Teaching Thinking.* Alexandria, VA: The Association for Supervision and Curriculum Development.

Sternberg, R. (1985). Teaching critical thinking, Part I: Are we making critical mistakes? *Phi Delta Kappan,* November.

EPILOGUE: BEHAVING CONSISTENTLY WITH OUR COGNITIVE GOALS AND OBJECTIVES

"What you do speaks so loudly, they can't hear what you say."

R. W. Emerson

∞   ∞   ∞

As educators we have great responsibility for instilling these modes of thinking and intelligent behaviors in our students. We must teach them to value intelligent, creative, and rational action. To do so, we must provide the conditions in which the intelligent behaviors can be practiced and demonstrated. We must believe that *all* students can grow in their ability to behave more intelligently. We must have faith that all humans can become more gifted people.

Finally, we must set an example by becoming models of these intelligent behaviors ourselves. Students are quick to identify the inconsistency between what a teacher verbalizes as ideal behavior and the demonstration of that behavior. Powerful teachers of thinking will constantly strive to bring their words, actions, beliefs, values, and goals for students into harmony.

Research in modeling substantiates that young people acquire much of their behavior, feelings, attitudes, and values, not through direct instruction, but rather through imitation of both adult and peer models (Bandura and Walter, 1973; Good and Brophy, 1973). A considerable number of studies bear out that students adopt new behavior patterns or modify their own behavior on the basis of observation alone. Thus, since there is such extended contact between teacher and student, the teacher is one of the most significant and influential models in the student's life.

Two Ways of Modeling

Modeling tends to reinforce students' perceptions of the values and goals proclaimed by the teacher or the school. One way to model is to overtly act out or demonstrate a behavior so students can see, hear, and experience it. Another, more subtle, way is to exemplify the desirable behaviors in the day-to-day interactions between students and adults. Although subtle, these interactions strongly influence students in those desired behavior patterns, actions, and reactions.

- If listening to one another is a target behavior in cognitive education, then teachers who listen to students will greatly enhance the probability of their achieving this objective.

- If solving problems in a rational, scientific manner is valued, when problems arise in the school or classroom, students must observe teachers and administrators solving problems in this manner (Belcher, 1975).

- If restraining impulsivity is a desired characteristic of intelligent problem solvers, then students must witness teachers and administrators reacting calmly and patiently during stressful situations.

- If teachers desire that students understand others' points of view, values, and differences (overcoming ego-centrism), then teachers will accept and strive to understand students' points of view and differences.

- If teachers want students to become enthusiastic about thinking, they must demonstrate enthusiasm about puzzles, challenges, and complex tasks (Rosenshine, 1970).

- If we are "do as I say, not as I do" type educators, then students will easily and quickly sense this incongruity between our behavior and our stated values. A "credibility gap" will develop. The end result can be hostility, frustration, and confusion.

In the last analysis, there is probably only one person whose behavior we have power to control, refine, and modify: *our own.*

References

Bandura, A. and Walter, R. (1963). *Social Learning and Personality Development*. New York: Holt, Rinehart and Winston.

Belcher, T. (1975). Modeling original divergent responses: An initial investigation. *Journal of Educational Research, 67,* 351-358.

Good, T. and Brophy, J. *Looking in Classrooms*. New York: Harper and Row.

Rosenshine, B. (1970). Enthusiastic teaching, a research review. *School Review, 78,* 279-301.